SOME PARTY IN HEAVEN

Through Trauma and Tragedy to Ultimate Triumph

NOEL DAVIDSON

SOME PARTY IN HEAVEN

Through Trauma and Tragedy to Ultimate Triumph

NOEL DAVIDSON

Ambassador International
Greenville, South Carolina & Belfast, Northern Ireland

www.ambassador-international.com

Some Party in Heaven
Through Trauma and Tragedy to Ultimate Triumph

Copyright 2012 - NOEL DAVIDSON
All rights reserved

ISBN: 978-1-62020-124-4
eISBN: 978-1-62020-176-3

Printed by Bethel Solutions

Ambassador International
Emerald House
427 Wade Hampton Blvd
Greenville, SC 29609, USA
www.ambassador-international.com

Ambassador Books and Media
The Mount
2 Woodstock Link
Belfast, BT6 8DD, Northern Ireland, UK
www.ambassadormedia.co.uk

The colophon is a trademark of Ambassador

Proceeds from the sale of this book will be used to further Christ's
Kingdom at home and abroad

Contents

INTRODUCTION

In the spring of 1994 I was invited to meet Hertford and Phyllis Arnold. A friend had told me about the personal tragedy which had come upon their family. I could scarcely believe that such a succession of heartbreak could occur in the same household.

Yet the idea of asking me to meet them was so I could hear their story, with a view to writing a book about it.

This couple must be totally devastated, I reckoned, before we met.

What can I say to them? Will what I have heard already not be too sad to include in a book? And that's not taking into account what I will hear from them. That was how I reasoned before we met, but my perspective changed completely in three hours one evening.

As we sat together after a meal in a Belfast restaurant, Phyllis produced a photograph album and wept freely as she recounted one family trauma after another.

Yet it wasn't all doom and gloom.

A sparkle could be seen in a tear-clouded eye.

"I'm sure you think I am making an awful fool of myself here," she apologised, "but we are so delighted that somebody is interested in telling our story. You see we believe these things happened to bring us to God and to strengthen our faith in Him. If a book is written about our lives we would want all the glory and praise to go to God, Who has brought us through this far."

I undertook to write their story to give praise to God and

started into a regular research pattern. Hertford and Phyllis came to visit Liz and me in our home in Larne, and we went to see them in their bungalow in Donacloney.

There were often tears as I heard, took notes of, and then began to write the touching story that was to become the first edition of this book.

The launch of 'Some Party in Heaven' on Friday, 17th November, 1995, was a memorable occasion. The function room in Malone House, Belfast, was crammed with people for the event, and there was hardly a dry eye in the building as Hertford and Phyllis relived their story.

Thousands of copies of that original version have been sold since then and it has, without doubt, accomplished Hertford and Phyllis's initial aim of our introductory day. It has brought glory and praise to God.

Many have been moved by it. Dozens have confessed to having 'cried all the way through it.' Others have been comforted, and some challenged. Learning of this response has been most reassuring for the young parents as they continue to travel across the province taking meetings in church and community groups.

An example of the most encouraging type of feedback of all was what happened to Phyllis a couple of months ago. She had spoken at a church group in Ballymena and while shaking hands with the congregation as they left, noticed a lady hanging back, as though wanting to have a word with her.

When most had left, the lady stepped forward, and taking Phyllis by the hand, said, with tears in her eyes, "I thought you might like to know that I was saved a few years ago when reading your book, 'Some Party in Heaven.'"

"That's wonderful!" Phyllis exclaimed. "That's why we had that book written. It was to bring glory to God, and hearing of people brought to the Saviour as a result of it gives us a special thrill."

It was now her turn to wipe away a tear. What she didn't tell the Ballymena convert was that she wasn't the first one she or Hertford had heard of who had come to the Lord through reading the book. There had been others before her, over the past 17 years.

As I have travelled around various church appointments over that period people have commented to me on 'Some Party in Heaven.' The remark usually runs something like, "One of your books that really touched me, and I remember so well, is 'the one with the balloons on the front.'"

This is invariably followed up with a query, "Why can we not get it now? It isn't in the bookshops anymore. Is it out of print?"

Hertford and Phyllis hear similar comments and encounter much the same questions as they continue to fulfil their busy schedule of speaking engagements. They, though, face additional enquiries, for they are frequently asked, "What about the boys in the book? Where are they now and what are they doing with themselves? Then there's the business, too. Did you ever move to that factory you were planning in Dromore?"

This updated edition will, we believe, perform two basic functions. Firstly it will allow the original 'Some Party in Heaven' readers, and others who have followed the story in 'Rejoice Always' magazine, to find out how God has continued to bless Hertford and Phyllis and their two surviving sons down the years.

It will also allow a totally new readership to experience the emotional roller-coaster that is the entire story. Just think – if you are 30 years old now, you were only 13 when the original version was published!

The above two I have described as 'basic functions.' The main and transcendent aim of the Arnold family, the publishers, and Liz and me, however, in seeing this enormously popular book republished is exactly the same as it was in 1995. It is just as Phyllis stated it, the very first day I met her, 'To bring praise and glory to God, Who has brought us through THIS far."

If you read it and come to faith in Christ, or if you are a Christian facing successive trials in life and are led into a deeper, fuller relationship with our loving caring God, then it will have fulfilled its purpose.

And what's more, you will be unbelievably blessed as well.

Noel I. Davidson
November 2012

Chapter 1

WILL YOU GO?

"If the Lord Jesus were to come right now, I wonder how many from this room would rise to meet Him?"

The voice of Hedley Murphy challenged the audience in a meeting in Moira, Co. Down. The atmosphere was solemn. Silent and still.

Young Phyllis Blakely glanced from side to side. She was almost seventeen years old. Her mother had persuaded her to go to the meeting, with her sister Gloria.

"It would please your uncle Eddie," she had coaxed.

As she observed those seated around her Phyllis came to the conclusion that most of them would 'rise to meet' Jesus if He were to come that moment. She knew them. Fine, Christian, meeting-going types the majority of them. They were all people of high moral standards and well-spoken of in the countryside.

Yes. They would mostly all rise.

Then there was Gloria, sitting beside her. Gloria was a good girl. Clean living, decent sort of person, perhaps a Christian, so she would probably go too.

That just left herself. When she came to close self-scrutiny the arrow of conviction embedded itself deep into her heart.

If the Lord Jesus were to come tonight, she wouldn't rise to meet Him.

It was as simple as that.

She wasn't ready.

She wasn't saved.

And she knew that perfectly well.

That knowledge made her determined. This was going to be the night. Phyllis was going to settle the matter, once and for all. And it was going to be tonight.

Sitting there she gradually lost all sense of her surroundings. She drifted into reverie.

Thoughts flooded back into her troubled mind.

Phyllis remembered the messages she had heard as a little child, in Kilmore Gospel Hall. That, in turn, made her think of the Mc Canns. How faithful they had been, collecting her every Sunday to take her to Sunday School.

Genuine Christians the Mc Canns. They would go when Jesus came. There was no doubt about that.

Still the verses, choruses and snippets of Bible stories continued to zip out of her memory bank and bombard her whirling brain. Reminiscence returned rapidly to reality, however, when the preacher's voice announced the final hymn.

"Let's sing in closing," he was saying, "When the trumpet of the Lord shall sound."

The congregation creaked stiffly into standing mode and began to sing lustily.

They seemed to sing with particular conviction the last line of each verse, repeated in the chorus, "When the roll is called up yonder I'll be there."

Phyllis didn't sing. She just prayed, inwardly, earnestly.

She was broken. Tears trickled down her cheeks.

"Lord, please don't come yet," she pleaded. "These people all believe they are going to be 'there.' I want to be 'there' too. O Lord, please don't come until I get saved!"

As the congregation filed out, Phyllis held back. She wanted to speak to the preacher. She needed help. Tonight was the night. Tuesday 17 February, 1981. This was it.

Mr. Hedley Murphy spoke to her gently. He read verses from the Bible. Many of them she recognised from having committed them to memory in Kilmore Gospel Hall Sunday School.

Then she prayed. It was a sincere prayer from the heart.

"Lord Jesus," she began, "I know I am a sinner. I need You to save and change me. I believe that You died on the cross to take away my sins. As I come to You now, please forgive my sin and make me Your own."

With that the burden of sin disappeared. There came a realization that she was saved.

It had been so simple to trust in Jesus.

A tremendous sense of peace enfolded her.

Phyllis just wished she could relive the end of the meeting so that she could sing with God-fearing gusto, along with all the others, "When the roll is called up yonder I'll be there!"

As she left the room, Uncle Eddie was waiting. He hadn't gone home. Stepping towards her and interpreting her smile as a happy harbinger, he said, "Well, Phyllis...?" It was half a statement but more a question.

Phyllis was radiant and confident by now.

"I got saved tonight, Uncle Eddie," she blurted out.

"Oh that's great!" Eddie Weir made no attempt to conceal his delight. "That's an answer to prayer. I have been praying that one of you Blakelys would soon get saved."

Phyllis was one of the Blakelys. There were seven of them. Besides Gloria who had come with her there were Heather, Alva, Jackson, Estlin and Linden.

Most of these others had also been asked to come, but they 'all with one consent began to make excuse.'

"I have to fix my car," claimed one.

"I have to see my girl-friend," said another.

"I've arranged to meet one of my mates in Lurgan at half-seven," was a third excuse. And so it went on.

But Phyllis and Gloria had gone. To please either mother or Uncle Eddie, or both.

Now Phyllis was saved, and this pleased them both. When her mother heard of the night's big event, she too rejoiced. Her pleasure was less exuberant, more self-controlled, than that of her Uncle Eddie, but genuine, nonetheless.

"You have made the right decision, Phyllis," she assured her daughter. "May God bless you."

By the time she arrived home from the meeting her dad knew as well. He stopped his radiant daughter as they met in the kitchen doorway. "You will never regret the decision you made tonight, Phyllis," were his simple words of encouragement.

Next morning at breakfast, however, Phyllis began to think her mother had changed her mind.

She began to probe, to question.

"Are you sure, Phyllis, that it wasn't just your emotions that overcame you last night?" she enquired.

Mothers know their daughters through and through. Ethel Blakely was no exception. She knew her Phyllis. She was an emotional girl, easily touched. Phyllis would be liable to react spontaneously in a highly-charged atmosphere.

"No, mother. This is no emotional thing. This is the real thing. I got saved last night. I got Jesus in my heart last night."

Mother was convinced. When she heard the new convert's calm declaration in the cold clear light of a new day, she was satisfied.

Her daughter would need some advice now, she knew.

"You will find, Phyllis," she began softly, "that the things that once interested you won't interest you as much anymore. And you will probably find, too, that your old friends won't want you so much either. But don't let that worry you. You have found the Saviour, and that is the most important thing in life. You will soon find new friends, with the same desires as yourself."

With that sensible counsel ringing in her ears, Phyllis set off for work.

When she arrived home in the evening Phyllis found that the 'New Christians Advice bureau' was ready to begin another session. With mother as adviser-in-chief.

The local Christian community was abuzz with the news. Family, friends and relations had been on the phone to Mrs. Blakely.

Then came the variety of advice...

"Tell her to seek out Christian friends," they said.

"Tell her to read her Bible every day," they said.

"Make sure she doesn't neglect her prayer times," they said.

Uncle Eddie's idea summarised them all.

"Eric Spence runs a prayer meeting and Bible study in his home in Hilllsborough every Wednesday evening. It would great if she could start going there," he suggested.

When Ethel Blakely told Phyllis of all those who had been ringing she was pleased. She hadn't really been aware that so many people could be so genuinely concerned about her.

After recounting all the recommendations she had recorded, mother finished up with Uncle Eddie's advice about the prayer meeting.

Phyllis didn't hesitate. Now that she was prepared to go to meet Jesus when He came, she could probably manage to make it to a prayer meeting in Hillsborough, she reckoned.

"Of course I'll go, mother!" was her immediate answer. "I'll start next week!"

And she did.

Her brother Alva's girlfriend, Marjorie, bought her a

little book called 'Sunrise to Sunset.' It contained a selection of daily readings by Derick Bingham and Phyllis was really blessed by that book. So eager was she to learn more about her newly-found faith that she read it not only from 'sunrise to sunset' but also half the night as well!

Gradually the babe-in-Christ began to show signs of growth. The desire for Scripture reading, prayer meetings and all things spiritual was increasing.

Phyllis couldn't understand it all herself. Before that hallowed night in Moira she used to think Christians were a crowd of stiff stooges, stuffed shirts and wet blankets. Having now become one herself though, she realised that had all been nonsense They were none of these things. At least she wasn't anyway!

It was great!

Going to and from the Wednesday evening prayer meeting, and many other times besides, Phyllis listened to a tape someone had given her. It was of hymns, sung by Rev. William McCrea.

As the little brown Mini, which her dad had bought her for her seventeenth birthday, sped on its way, it reverberated to the strains of, 'Worthy is the Lamb,' Will the Circle Be Unbroken?' and other well known hymns. Often, Rev. McCrea had the accompaniment of Phyllis as she sang along, beating out time on the steering wheel!

Phyllis felt so close to the Saviour on those occasions that she used to commune with Him as she travelled along.

"Lord, I just feel You sitting there beside me," she would say, in hushed tones. "I can't see You I know, but I can feel You close to me. Thank You. Thank You. Thank You, Lord!"

Chapter 2
YOU ARE MINE, AREN'T YOU?

The Arnold brothers, Hertford and Tyrrell, were interested in fast cars. They spent most of their spare time either racing their cars or taking them to bits and putting them together again, all in an attempt to coax a few more miles-per-hour out of well-worn engines.

The Blakely brothers, Jackson and Estlin, also spent a high percentage of their time following motor-sport. This mutual interest led to a bond of friendship developing between Hertford and Tyrrell, the road racers, and the Blakely fast car enthusiasts. They attended all the race meetings together, though some of them possibly enjoyed the social side of the sport as much as they did the thrills and spills of the track. Discussing the performance of the cars over a few beers in a bar was as satisfying to them as hearing the deafening roar of the engines and the squeal of tortured, smoking rubber.

Hertford's obsession with cars and tinkering with them, led to him becoming a frequent visitor to the Blakely home.

After a few months Jackson and Estlin began to suspect that their friend was interested in more than revs-per-minute. Something was happening to his own heartbeat they reckoned. They said nothing, though. Time would tell.

They were to be proved correct. Hertford was beginning to cast admiring glances towards their sister, Phyllis. He wasn't hard to persuade to slide out from below an engine, and put the spanner down, when she came out into the yard to chat to all the lads.

One evening, just before he left for home, Hertford dashed into the kitchen where Phyllis was, and said, "I would like to take you out some night next week, Phyllis, if that's OK. Any night you like."

Her two brothers, who had been brushed aside, then totally ignored, as Hertford made his first date with Phyllis, nodded and winked at each other. They knew this would happen. They had seen it coming for weeks.

Phyllis pretended to look amazed.

Then she looked really pleased.

An uncontrollable blush glowed on her cheek.

"That would be nice," she replied, shyly.

Unknown to him, she rather fancied this strong, frank and friendly fellow who appeared to be coming about their household more and more. The most trivial matter seemed to have given him an excuse to call round.

Now she knew why! But she wasn't complaining!

So it was arranged. They went out together the following Wednesday evening and enjoyed it. Something 'clicked.' They found they liked each other, and had common interests.

The next step was to meet again. And they did, the next Wednesday evening. Thus it went on.

A pattern became established. Every Wednesday evening and most Saturday evenings, they met.

There was one difficulty, though. This single complication highlighted a particular area where Hertford, and his new girlfriend, Phyllis, did not share a common interest.

Wednesday was the evening of the prayer meeting and Bible study. As Phyllis began to fall in love with Hertford, she began to cool down towards the Lord.

When the racing season finished, and autumn days grew shorter, the young couple began to spend more time in the pubs and dances than beside the track.

Phyllis never felt at ease in these places. She was happy in
Hertford's company.

Yes, increasingly so.

She wasn't happy in the haunts where she often found
herself, just to be in his company.

No, increasingly no.

"This is not right!" her spiritual conscience claimed with
alarming frequency, as she heard the name of her Lord being
taken in vain. "You shouldn't be in here!"

When she mentioned it to Hertford, he just laughed at her.

"Can we not just go for a drive or a walk, or sit in and
watch TV or something?" she would ask every now and again.
"I don't like the crowd in those pubs we go to. I'm saved you
know."

"What, so you mean you're 'saved'?" he would jibe. "You
were always a decent-living girl, Phyllis. You don't need all
that kind of stuff. Neither do I, for that matter."

Thus Phyllis became the centre of a spiritual tug-of-war.

On one side, it appeared, grabbing one wrist, holding
tightly and pulling hard was Hertford, whom she loved dearly.

On the opposite, holding the other wrist, and pulling
gently but firmly was her Lord, whom she also loved dearly.

"I loved you so much that I died for you, Phyllis. You are
mine," He was saying.

Phyllis was sure she was going to be spiritually pulled in
two. There was always this constant contest.

Hertford versus the Lord. The Lord versus Hertford.

Gradually the winner emerged. Phyllis had stopped
attending her weekly Bible study when she met Hertford.
Now her personal Bible study was becoming more erratic.

Regular precious prayer times gave place to hurried
shopping lists to God when things weren't going too great.

Rev. William Mc Crea's tape was tucked away, unheard,

into a side pocket of the Mini, where it kept company with a duster, a dried up chamois and a can of de-icer with a cracked cap.

They had just been 'going out' with each other for seven weeks when Hertford made a sudden proposal one Saturday evening.

The evening had gone well and the warmth of the love that was shared between them was becoming more evident. This was the right time for the big one, he was sure.

"Phyllis, I love you and I want to marry you," he stated quite simply. "How about us getting engaged at Christmas?"

She just couldn't believe it! Phyllis was pleased and thrilled, stunned and speechless all at once. Surely this was only the drink talking. Hertford had downed a pint or two that evening.

When she reined in her runaway thoughts, she expressed the doubts that clouded her delight, to her would-be husband. You don't really mean it, Hertford," she began. "You don't know what you are talking about! Sure we have only been going together for six or seven weeks!"

"I do know what I'm talking about! And I do mean it!" was Hertford's instinctive, insistent reply.

Phyllis needed time. She just had to think this whole matter through.

"OK Hertford. OK, I believe you," she conceded. "But this is important you know. I need time to think about it. You have sprung this all on me so suddenly! Ask me tomorrow night and I'll tell you!"

Hertford Arnold was a young man of purpose. He liked instant answers and immediate action. No hanging about or messing around. Waiting was not one of his strong points.

He agreed, reluctantly. "Right," he declared. "I will be here tomorrow night at eight o'clock. Will you promise to answer me then?"

"I will, I promise," Phyllis assured him.

With that they kissed, and parted.

As soon as she got into the house Phyllis rushed up to her bedroom. Throwing off her coat and kicking off her shoes, she launched herself across the bed. She landed in a half-prostrate, half-praying position, and there she remained.

"Lord," she prayed in turmoil," if Hertford Arnold is the man for me, please let me know. And if he's not, drive him away from me, somehow. Lord, please show me what to do. I need to know Your will for me, Lord. And I need to know it before eight o'clock tomorrow night!"

Still there was the struggle. She was trying to please the Lord, and love Hertford.

Now he had gone and complicated the whole issue by asking her to marry him!

Sunday seemed unending.

For Phyllis it was a trying-to-make-your-mind-up kind of day. Gazing out the window she wondered, "What should I do?"

Picking at her meals she wondered, "What should I say?"Barely a single word of the general babbling of the busy Blakely household banter registered with her as she wondered, "What am I going to tell him?"

As the day progressed, the answer came. She began to listen to her heart. Just as the early morning mist burns away with the heat of the sun, slowly revealing the surrounding landscape, so the picture became clearer, bit by bit.

When Hertford drove into the yard, spot on eight o'clock, in his father's grey Granada, Phyllis was waiting. She hopped in beside him.

"Well, what's your answer to what I asked you last night?" was Hertford's immediate question. There was no, "You're looking well tonight, love," or "Nice night, isn't it?"

Direct as ever, her impatient boyfriend came straight to the point.

"You remember, Phyllis, I asked you last night if you would marry me? You promised me you would tell me tonight. Well, I'm waiting... what's your answer?"

Phyllis threw herself across into his arms.

"Yes! Yes! Yes!" she replied, repeatedly.

The young couple hugged each other in ecstasy. They believed now they were meant for each other.

"There's just one small problem, though," Phyllis brought them both down to earth, when she regained her breath.

A fleeting shadow crossed Hertford's face. He was worried, but only slightly, and only momentarily.

"What's your small problem?" he enquired.

"I think Christmas would be too soon to get engaged," she explained. "Daddy would have a fit if we ever mentioned it. Could we leave it off for a bit? Say, to my birthday?"

Hertford agreed to that. After all, her birthday, he knew, was only a little over two months after Christmas.

So, just to emphasise the genuine nature of his intentions, Hertford bought Phyllis a gold watch for Christmas.

The engagement ring came on her eighteenth birthday, 7th March, 1982.

Chapter 3
HAPPY DAYS

The wedding of Hertford and Phyllis on 23rd April, 1983, in High Street Presbyterian Church, Lurgan, was a happy occasion. In addition to the joining together of two loving hearts, it afforded an opportunity for the coming together of two large families.

As wedding days so often are for parents, it was a day of joy, tinged with just a hint of sadness for Tom and Ethel Blakely and Ford and Jean Arnold. They were pleased at the prospects for their children, but conscious of a gap looming up somewhere ahead for themselves.

Brothers and sisters of the bride and groom assisted in every possible way to make the 'big day' a success. Some were in the bridal party, others acted as ushers at the church, and all the remainder attended with their husbands or wives, boyfriends or girlfriends, contributing much to the overall happiness of the event. They all enjoyed themselves, basking in the warmth of the infectious love of Hertford and Phyllis.

After the wedding, the young couple moved into the Arnold family home. Hertford's parents had built a new house, leaving theirs for the newly-weds.

It was a good house, a solid country house. The main feature of their new abode was the massive kitchen with its great terrazzo floor, white Aga, and huge twelve foot by five foot table.

This gigantic table, their dominant item of furniture, proved to be the setting for some heart-to-heart conversations between the young couple.

Hertford sat at one end of the long table.

His new wife was seated just around the corner, beside him.

Often, when a meal was finished they would push the empty plates away from them and look at one another, then up at the length of the table. They would ponder, and dream and chat.

Regardless of the topic on which the conversation started, it always seemed to end up on a constantly recurring theme. It was about a family. Their family. The family that they hoped so much they were going to have.

"How long do you think it will be until we have a family big enough to fill every chair?" one would ask.

"Ten or twelve years, likely, unless we have a set or two of twins!" would come the reply.

"How many boys do you think there will be?"

"How many girls?"

Thus the question and answer fantasy sessions continued, fuelled by much love and punctuated by much laughter. These end-of-the-table, end-of-a-meal, affectionate exchanges reflected an ambition of both husband and wife.

They had both come from large, happy families. They would both like to have a large, happy family.

They were overjoyed, then, a few months later, when Phyllis discovered she was expecting a baby. Their dream had taken at least its first tiny step towards fulfilment.

During those days of early married life, Phyllis was vaguely conscious of God. She used to pray to Him, but only sometimes, and usually only when something was troubling her.

She had lost her Christian conscience as well. Things that once caused raging storms of guilt to buffet her burdened soul didn't even create the faintest ripple now.

Anyway, she had something else to occupy her mind. There was someone else to talk about, to plan for. Her Saviour was shoved back into a distant third place in the race for her priority thinking.

Sitting side by side before the Aga many an evening, often with the lower oven door open and their feet jammed into it for heat, Hertford and she would discuss the baby-to-come.

"What room should we do up for him or her?" was one topic of discussion. Other matters considered at some length ranged from prams and cots to toys and nappies.

Everything for little junior was going to be of the very best they could afford. It was important to them. They were ever so content.

Just one thing Hertford didn't like. It was being left on his own, at work on the farm, while Phyllis attended her antenatal clinic. Time dragged when she was away.

On her return the anxious husband was invariably waiting in the yard. In his own direct, but caring manner, he would enquire, "Well, how are you today? What had the doctor to say about the both of you?"

Then they would go into the house, put the kettle on the Aga, and Phyllis would give him a detailed, word-by-word account of what the doctor had said about her condition.

When he was satisfied that all concerned were fit and well, and Phyllis kept assuring him that the doctor had told her they were, Hertford would return to work. That was usually about half-an-hour and two cups of coffee later!

Christmas, 1983, was a joyful time for the young couple. It was their first Christmas together. As she decorated the tree in the corner of the living room, Phyllis remarked to her devoted husband, "Just think, Hertford, next Christmas there will be three of us. We will have a baby to share all this with!"

On New Year's Day, 1984, a Sunday, the happily expectant

couple had lunch with Hertford's parents. In the afternoon Phyllis was admitted to Lagan Valley Hospital, Lisburn.

Again she found herself coping with that mixed-feeling sensation. She didn't really relish the prospect of giving birth to her firstborn, but she did look forward to having a baby of her own to nurse.

As Phyllis lay in her hospital bed she prayed about it. Although the fire of her faith had long since faded to a flicker, she communed with her Lord about what lay ahead. "Lord, please help me in the coming days," she would pray, and always there was the same conclusion, the final request. "And please, Lord, let my baby be born safely,"

On Thursday 5th January, 1984, her prayers were answered. Thomas Jackson Arnold was born, called after his Granda Blakely.

He was some baby, too, tipping the scales at eleven pounds seven and a half ounces! The news spread like wildfire through the maternity unit. Some of the canteen staff visited the ward as they went off duty. "We just called in to see this big fellow so we could measure him up for his school uniform!" they joked.

The interest of the hospital staff, however, didn't in any way match the delight of his mother and father. They were parents now, and proud of it!

Hertford rang everybody whom he thought would be even remotely interested. He was so thrilled! The family circles on both sides were overjoyed as well. Everyone loved the young couple, and they all knew of their desire for a sizeable family.

Thomas was a sturdy start to their campaign.

Phyllis, the radiant mother, just glowed. When she wasn't actually nursing the baby out of the cot, she was watching him in it, or rearranging the rapidly increasing collection of flowers, toys and teddies around it.

On the day she was told she could go home, it snowed heavily.

Phyllis phoned her husband.

"We can go home, Hertford!" she exclaimed excitedly. "Can you come for me? Even if you have to hire a helicopter, can you bring us home?"

Hertford's days in motor-sport hadn't been wasted after all. He knew a trick or two about driving in all conditions. A foot of snow wouldn't deter him from fetching his wife and infant son home!

"Don't worry about a thing Phyllis," he assured her. "If they are going to let you home, we will surely get you home!"

Phyllis loved her Hertford's determination. She was pleased with his decision. Above everything else, she wanted to be back at home with her husband and their little baby boy.

Tyrell came with Hertford and they made it to the Hospital although the roads were well covered with snow. What an exciting homecoming!

Driving back up the M1 through deep snow, in the red EscortXR3, Tyrell had a big responsibility. The conditions were bad and the cargo was precious.

Phyllis nursed baby Thomas.

Hertford's attention was divided. It was a three-way split. He was either concentrating on the hazardous conditions, his wife, now a mother, or their little baby son.

Before leaving for the Hospital, Hertford had stoked up the fire. And what a fire! The living room was like an oven when they entered it. The tiles on the hearth were too hot to touch, and the chimney breast creaked in agony.

It was bitter winter weather, and his wife and son were definitely not going to be frozen in a cold house!

The warmth of their arrival was to herald happy days to come.

The resounding echo had gone from the kitchen now.

Nappies, a baby bath, a carry-cot and sterilizing units

were the additional items of essential equipment. Objects of various sizes, shapes and colours that either shook, rattled or squeaked were the ornaments.

The big table always had something sitting on it.

Hertford remarked once that it took more space for baby Thomas, with all his bits and pieces, 'and all the size of him too,' than it did for Phyllis and him put together.

A new member of the Arnold household had come home.

Things were never going to be quite the same again!

Chapter 4
OH NO!

Baby Thomas brought much delight to many. He was the centre of attention in the family circle.

The entire lifestyle of his young parents was readjusted to accommodate his needs. Programmes of work, snatched moments of leisure, and even the extent of any night's sleep were geared to fit in with his feeding, sleeping, waking and resting patterns.

It was quite a change for Hertford, who once believed that you worked hard by day and slept soundly at night, to be standing perched on one leg by the Aga, at two o'clock in the morning heating a bottle. The other foot was being kept warm in the bottom oven. A terrazzo floor was desperately cold on the bare feet!

Thomas's grandparents on both sides and his new aunts and uncles kept calling at the house or ringing up, to enquire about him.

"Well, how's the big man today?" they would ask.

Phyllis's sister Heather, however, had a keen interest in babies in general, and two in particular, at that time. She had just had a baby herself, a girl with a shock of black hair, called Carolyn.

As Carolyn was her second child, Heather felt herself qualified by experience to help and advise Phyllis, a novice, in matters relating to the care of her infant son.

One afternoon in mid-March 1984, Phyllis went round to Heather's house in Dromore for a chat. As always she had Thomas in his carry-cot.

Hertford was busy in the fields, preparing to sow the barley. It was a pleasant, warming-up type of an early spring day. The first of the daffodils were beginning to reveal a hint of yellow. It was the sort of an afternoon when the days of winter faded from the memory. There was life in the air. And hope.

The two mothers and sisters sat in Heather's kitchen and fed their babies. They chatted animatedly to one another as the bottles were emptied. Something Phyllis noticed, though, caused her a little concern. She had observed it before but hadn't mentioned it to anyone. Thomas was always slow to finish his bottles. Carolyn, who was a month younger, usually had hers scoffed in half the time.

As Heather placed the empty bottle on the table, and straightened her baby up, 'to get up her wind,' Phyllis exclaimed, "She couldn't have finished already!"

'She couldn't.' But she had.

When the feeding session was over, Phyllis and Heather went into the living room for a leisurely gossip. They would allow their babies to stretch and kick. It would be a refreshing time for them all.

Heather was on her knees on the floor, adjusting the change mats, and making sure the children were comfortable. She had her back to Phyllis who was sitting on the settee.

Trying to sound as casual as possible, the mildly concerned mother asked the question which had begun to niggle her. "Heather, do you not notice a difference between Thomas and Carolyn?"

Heather didn't turn round, didn't look up. She just answered, "What do you mean, Phyllis?"

Before explaining exactly what it was she meant, Phyllis stood up. Then looking tenderly down at her cherished little boy as he lay flat on the floor, she blurted it out.

"Do you not think there is something wrong with Thomas,

Heather?" she asked quickly. The words seemed to explode from her mouth like fizz from a well-shaken drink can. She had to get it over with.

Now it was out. What would be the reaction?

Nothing at first.

There was an awkward, almost embarrassing, silence. Both sisters felt strange.

It was creepy.

Slowly Heather turned round and looked up at her younger sister. Phyllis noticed that her eyelashes and cheeks were glinting-wet.

"To tell you the truth, Phyllis," she replied gently, "Mummy is worried about Thomas. You know she has had seven of us so she should have some idea of what she is talking about. She thinks Thomas's head should be a lot firmer by now than what it is."

Turning back down again to attend to the children, Heather hastily brushed the tears from her cheeks with the side of her hand.

So that was it! Phyllis's worst fears had been realised. There WAS a difference between the two babies.

Both sisters wept unashamedly.

Now that it was all out in the open, they could talk about it. They could act on it too. Changing infants back and forward between them they compared their firmness. This exercise progressed to a comparison of every possible feature they could think of.

Now that she had confided her blackest fears to her sister, Phyllis became more emotionally distressed. Heather kept trying to console her. She assured her younger sister that if there was a difference, there would probably be some perfectly simple medical explanation for it.

"Just you stay here with me," Heather suggested. "My

doctor will be calling this afternoon to see Carolyn. We will ask him what he thinks."

The next car to pull up at the house, however, was not the family GP. It was Ethel Blakely, the young mothers' mother! "What on earth is wrong with the pair of you?" she asked as soon as she entered the living room. It didn't take her many seconds to size up the situation. Red eyes, and soggy hankies in clenched fists, were the sure giveaways.

"What's the truth of all this, mummy?" Phyllis came straight to the point, addressing her bewildered mother. "Do you think there is something the matter with Thomas?"

Mrs. Blakely stood still. She looked across from Heather to Phyllis. Then down from Thomas to Carolyn. She needed thinking time. How was she going to handle this one? How was she going to tell her daughter what she really thought?

"Yes, Phyllis," she began lovingly. "I think his wee head should be firmer by now."

She paused for breath, but noticing the just-about-to-cry-again look on her young daughter's face, went on hastily, "But don't panic. I would advise you to take Thomas to the doctor and ask him to conduct a thorough examination."

"Well, actually, I have just told Phyllis to wait until my doctor calls this afternoon. I will ask if he would have a look at Thomas," Heather informed her mother.

Mrs. Blakely was glad to hear that. "Good idea," she said. "I will just stay too and hear what his opinion is."

When the family doctor called, about an hour later, Heather met him in the kitchen. There was a whispered conversation. As they approached the living room door, Phyllis could hear, through the chink that had been left open, Heather preparing the doctor for what he might find.

"She is in here. She is really upset."

When the visiting GP entered the living room Phyllis

was cradling her treasured Thomas protectively in her arms.

Speaking quietly, he instructed Phyllis to lay him down on the floor. Then, kneeling down beside the baby, the doctor tried to lift him up.

As she watched him examine Thomas, Phyllis was conscious of little things which she had noticed before, but hadn't dared mention.

They didn't seem like little things now!

His head was floppy. Thomas could make no effort either to raise it up, or hold it up.

After completing an examination of the tiny arms and legs as well, the doctor agreed that, yes, he should probably be firmer by now. Realising the emotional state Phyllis was in, but also the medical implications of the baby's condition, he spoke kindly to the anxious mother.

"I would advise you to go, with Hertford, and take Thomas to see your own doctor as soon as possible," he counselled.

Phyllis had to wait until after the doctor had checked up on Carolyn, before leaving. Beyond that she couldn't stay. "I must go home and find Hertford," she said, through her tears, to her mother and sister.

Finding Hertford didn't prove difficult. When the work in the fields was finished for the day he started to clear out a sheugh on the lane. That way he could occupy his restless hands and brain and he would be in a position to greet his wife and son when they arrived home in time for tea.

He was pleased to recognise the engine noise at last. That was them coming now.

When Phyllis pulled up beside him she wound down the window. It didn't take more than one glance into the car at her to establish that all was not well.

"What's wrong with you?" he asked.

"There's nothing wrong with me, but I think there is

something wrong with Thomas," came the shock reply.

"What do you mean?" Hertford rushed to enquire. He was stunned.

"Let's both go down to the house and we can talk about it," his wife proposed in a voice that trembled with emotion.

Work was finished for good now. Shouldering the shovel and the fork, Hertford followed the car, which had set off in a flurry of stones and dust, to the house.

When the car drove into the yard, Hertford's mother came over to it. As Phyllis opened the door to get out, her mother-in-law asked, out of friendly interest, "Well, have you had a good day?"

Phyllis dissolved into tears. Again.

With that sickening sense of having said the wrong thing, Mrs. Arnold followed up with a considerate, "Is there something the matter with you, Phyllis?"

Opening another door of the car to lift Thomas out, the distraught young mother pointed to her infant son and said, through her sobs, "Not with me. But with him."

Jean Arnold's face turned ashen pale.

The two women carried Thomas into the kitchen and were soon followed by Hertford.

When she had spread the change mat out on the large kitchen table, Phyllis laid Thomas down on it. Then she copied what the doctor had done. She raised him gently.

"Look at his head," she kept repeating. "Look at his head."

When her awestruck husband and his numbed mother did as she asked, they saw what she meant. Thomas couldn't hold his head up. It just wobbled about. Or hung down limply.

Mrs. Arnold knew they had to do something. There was no point in just standing there all afternoon, becoming more dejected. "Hertford, you go and get changed," she ordered calmly. "Then the pair of you take Thomas down to the doctor's right away."

It was sensible advice. The only obvious course of action.

In twenty minutes the three of them were in the doctor's waiting room. Although they hadn't to wait any more than ten minutes it seemed like an eternity to Phyllis. She felt that all the others in there were staring at her.

They weren't, but she thought they were.

She felt that everybody knew her baby 'wasn't right.'

They didn't, but she thought they did.

If they all knew, why, oh why, hadn't somebody told her? Why had she not even caught it on herself before now? It was a horrible sensation.

When the family doctor examined Thomas he was aware that Phyllis was jumping to all kinds of conclusions, possibly with some justification.

To clarify a potentially very worrying situation for everyone he made an appointment at the Lagan Valley Hospital in Lisburn. Here Thomas would be seen by the gynaecologist who had attended his birth, and a paediatrician.

Hertford and Phyllis returned home, still perplexed, but with the minor consolation that somebody else was going to advise them about their little Thomas. When the young parents attended that appointment in the Lagan Valley Hospital, about two weeks later, the gynaecologist spoke to them first.

"I will always remember the day Thomas was born," he remarked. "There was great excitement in here."

"Yes, I remember that day well too!" Phyllis replied, struggling to force a smile. "We are worried that there is something wrong with Thomas, though."

Neither she nor her husband could have been prepared for the doctor's response.

"To be honest, we suspected there was something the matter with Thomas, but we couldn't be absolutely sure. There was so much joy in both of your hearts we thought it best to allow you to take him home. We knew if there was a problem with him it would become more evident with the passing of time and you would then realise it yourselves," he admitted.

Hertford and Phyllis were dumbfounded. They just sat and stared at each other and then at baby Thomas, totally speechless.

"There is a paediatrician here, an expert in children's ailments," the doctor went on consolingly. "Don't be worrying yourself unduly. Thomas is a lovely little boy. Everything possible will be done for him."

The examination of Thomas by the paediatrician was the most thorough to date. He tried to lift Thomas up, and observed his head movements. He worked with his arms and legs and tested his hands and feet.

Throughout the examination Phyllis kept firing questions. She was so uptight she was desperate to hear what the expert thought. And sooner would be better that later.

"What do you think?" she would ask.

"Can this be treated?" she would enquire.

While the examinations were being carried out, however, she got no answers. The paediatrician was intent on his work. He had to be sure of his diagnosis before he spoke.

When he did eventually comment it was merely to tell Hertford and Phyllis that he would like Thomas to be seen by a specialist in the Royal Victoria Hospital in Belfast. He would arrange the appointment.

Thus the waiting, the worrying, the uncertainty, dragged on.

The specialist paediatrician in the Royal Victoria Hospital had Thomas admitted so that extensive tests could be carried out.

It was early June, and hot summer weather. It was great

weather for farmers but Hertford barely noticed it. Indeed spring had merged into summer, but for Hertford and Phyllis one long anxious day had just blurred into the next. The type of weather, or the time of day or night, had become an irrelevance to them.

Thomas, and his condition, had become an obsession.

On a Friday, in the middle of the month, after all the results had been collated, Hertford and Phyllis met the specialist to hear the outcome. The final diagnosis.

"The scan has shown that a tiny part of the cerebellum is missing from Thomas' brain," the consultant explained. That was the medical, technical bit.

Then came the hard part, the knock-out blow.

"As a result of this Thomas will neither be able to walk nor talk nor sit up unaided. He will be both physically and mentally handicapped."

The young couple were devastated.

Their eyes were open, but they were seeing nothing.

Their legs had suddenly become weak and shaky. They were too numb to cry.

"We will want to monitor his development. We will arrange another appointment for six weeks' time" the specialist paediatrician said, in a soft tone little louder than a whisper, before slipping silently from the room. It hadn't been easy for her either.

Hertford and Phyllis were left with their baby, their tangled thoughts and their heavy hearts. They were both weeping now.

When they regained sufficient composure to allow them to return to the car, it was like an oven. The summer sun was blazing down. Thomas was placed into the back seat in his carry-cot.

The shattered parents still hadn't spoken a word to each other. They didn't know what to say. What could they say that would make any sense?

As the drive homeward began, Phyllis was besieged by a guilt complex.

'God is punishing you, Phyllis,' her thoughts accused. 'He has given you this baby because you have gone and married an unsaved man. You have backslidden and let Him down. You know what the Bible says, 'Don't be unequally yoked with unbelievers...'

Only sobs stirred the stillness. Their shared but silent sorrow was finding an emotional escape.

Hertford drove along with his elbow resting on the edge of the open window. As soon as one cigarette was finished he lit up another. Smoke drifted into the car and out into the shimmering heat.

His thoughts were about the rotten luck of it all.

'Four months ago I had a son and heir,' he mused. 'But now what have I got? And worse still, what can I do about it? If I could turn every sod on the farm into gold I still couldn't change a single thing.'

They both so loved their little Thomas, who knew nothing of their distress. He was sleeping peacefully in the back seat.

The young parents both felt so sick. They felt in some way 'let down' by somebody or something. Neither of them was quite sure by whom, or by what. It was going to be hard to talk about, too. How were they going to tell everybody?

It was Phyllis who spoke first, when they were almost home. Her opening remark was a kick-back against God.

"Why? Why? Why" she agonised. "How could there be a God who could let something like this happen?"

Hertford had no time whatsoever for God.

"What are you talking about GOD for?" he retorted fiercely, more from frustration than anger. "What has HE got to do with anything?"

Chapter 5
COMING TO TERMS

When they arrived home that Friday evening Hertford and Phyllis each contacted their parents who had been waiting anxiously for news.

On hearing the final result as described by the hospital paediatrician, and sensing how upset their children were, Tom and Ethel Blakely and Ford and Jean Arnold came down to the house immediately. They wanted to hear everything, every single word, the doctors had said. They didn't want to miss a thing.

Hertford and Phyllis found a sense of relief in pouring out their hearts to their sympathetic parents. It was great to release their pent-up emotions into understanding ears.

Everyone was so sad. So sorry. The muted conversations lasted on into the evening and then on into the night. Nobody wanted to go home. Nobody wanted to go to bed.

Everybody felt they should say something but were never quite sure of what would be a suitable or sensible thing to say. Conversations consisted of clipped sentences interspersed by sighs and tears. Many cups of tea were poured, only to remain half-drunk and cold. Nibbled biscuits lay around.

There was a strange eerie feeling about the house. It was as though something had just started to die. It was like finding the first petals of a treasured rose bloom lying rain-spattered in the mud.

In the weeks that followed Hertford and Phyllis went through the trauma of explaining the situation about Thomas to their wide circle of family and friends. They seemed to relive that hot June afternoon in 'the Royal' at least once every day. It came to the stage that it was like a drama which they had performed so often that they knew it perfectly. Both of them had their own particular lines off by heart. The acquired ability to recount the story in its most minute detail didn't bring any consolation, however. Each explanation was an emotional trial.

It was the care and sympathy of friends and family which meant so much to the young parents. They all loved Thomas. They doted on him.

As the sense that they were being borne along by the genuine, heartfelt concern of others enveloped Phyllis and Hertford, they gradually, slowly, came to terms with the word, and concept, 'handicapped.' It had not been easy. It was like recovering from a long and debilitating illness.

Things steadily began to return to normal. Normality meant something different now, though.

Hertford was back in the yard and on the tractor but he felt compelled to make little excursions back to the house every now and again. He just had to check that his wife and son were both OK. Perhaps he expected there to be a dramatic and sudden improvement in Thomas's condition. A miracle perhaps?

It didn't occur.

For Phyllis, normality meant adapting to a new routine, an entirely different lifestyle.

Her little Thomas had to be taken each week to Craigavon hospital to be exercised. These weekly visits to hospital proved to be a double benefit to her.

Firstly, she realised that she didn't have the only physically and mentally handicapped baby in Northern Ireland. There were others, just like Thomas. Other parents were coping with the same dilemma. This was comforting.

The second way in which these hospital appointments helped her was that she came in contact with well-informed and caring nursing staff. They always had time for her. She was able to pour out her heart to them. She could share all her worries and concerns, however minor.

Phyllis always received a kind and considerate response to all her queries. This made her feel better. Indeed she began to get the impression that she was in a certain sense privileged to have a child like Thomas so that she could learn all these things.

Putting on a brave face in public was what Hertford and Phyllis discovered to be by far their greatest challenge. Taking Thomas to visit friends, especially those who had normal children, was tough at first. They faced up to it with a smile on a quivering lip. The eye that sparkled with pride was occasionally misted by a tear.

People were really understanding. It was never so painful, second time round. Thus when the young parents began to recognise that Thomas was accepted for just who he was, by family and friends, they felt more content. It inspired a degree of confidence in the flagging, flattened soul.

Hertford and Phyllis had to be happy for Thomas. They couldn't be anything else, after the initial shock and then the gradual coming to terms, for he in himself was such a happy child.

Wrapped up in his own little world, Thomas was oblivious to the anxieties of the world of adults. He just chuckled and bubbled his way through every day, blissfully unaware of the concern of his loving parents and interested family circle.

When they had become reconciled to the fact that Thomas would always be unable to do the things most other children did, but that he was special, very special, in his own particular way, a question cropped up in the mind of his parents.

They were both worried about it as individuals. Then they shared it with each other. The medical profession assured them they shouldn't have any need to worry about it.

That didn't stop them being apprehensive all the same.

Often, as they lifted their baby, or fed him, or drove him to or from his exercise sessions, it drifted like a bad dream into, and around, their minds. It threatened to destroy their shared vision of a big happy family round a big homely table.

It was simply this.

Could it happen again?

Chapter 6
FORD

The deepest misgivings of Hertford and Phyllis were soon to be put to the test. In late summer 1984 Phyllis found out she was expecting a second baby.

Now the anxiety really began in earnest.

This was in spite of telling themselves that it probably wouldn't happen again. "Not so soon, surely," was a phrase they used often.

Still they worried.

It was also despite repeated medical assurances that the chances of having another handicapped baby were 'one in a million.'

Still they worried.

Having learnt to cope with all of Thomas's special needs they loved him dearly. Inwardly, secretly, however, they longed for another child who would fulfil a dual role.

Their hope was that the new addition to their family would be good company for Thomas. That would be very important. Secondly, they would just appreciate it so much if he or she could be like everybody else's babies seemed to be, physically and mentally normal.

No exercise sessions. No special diets. No particular demands of any kind. Just normal.

As the year progressed, so did Thomas. He was growing steadily and had started to feed better, provided everything was well mashed down. He couldn't manage big bites or large lumps.

He was now accepted by everybody. All his relatives had a 'soft spot' for him, probably because of his disability. His young parents were becoming daily more confident in dealing with his requirements. When Christmas 1984 came, Phyllis remembered her prediction of the previous year.

Yes. There were three of them now. She had been right about that.

Yes. They did have a baby to share everything with. She had been right about that as well.

There were, however, ways in which the reality of Christmas 1984 differed from the idyllic mental picture which had helped gild Christmas 1983.

Thomas was eleven months old, but he couldn't sit up, or crawl. He couldn't even hold his head up. In seasons of silent reflection doubts about his progress and his future prospects, whatever they were, would sneak stealthily into her mind. The young mother couldn't entertain them, though. Ignoring the occasional aching at her heart, which could easily have translated into bitterness, or even rejection, she tried ever so hard to think positively. She had to.

And what a joy it brought.

Christmas 1984 was a happy time for all three of them. Hertford and Phyllis made sure of that. Thomas meant so much to them. They would do everything to ensure he was comfortable and content.

Then there was this other baby to come. What would he or she be like?

Contemplating the birth of their second child brought mixed feelings. It was a restrained pleasure, like being forced to stifle a hearty sneeze. They were both excited and scared all at once.

Time, as it so often does, brought the answer to their uncertainty, an end to all the edgy speculation.

On 29th April 1985, their second baby, another boy, was born in Craigavon Hospital.

A few minutes after his birth, a doctor came out of the theatre and assured Hertford that this recent addition to their family was completely normal. "He is a great little boy. He is as strong as a bull," was his exact description.

About ten minutes later a nurse brought the infant out for Hertford to see. When he saw the little bundle of humanity pulling up his legs and waving his arms about, he realised what the doctor had said was true. He was witnessing it now with his own wondering eyes.

What a relief to the anxious father. All the worry of the past nine months seemed to evaporate in a split second. He was walking on air!

When Phyllis came round from sedation and was told her baby was normal, she could hardly believe it. It was brilliant.

Could it really be true? Like her husband before her, she needed convincing.

Proof was at hand, by a hand.

The gynaecologist came into the ward, and placing the new baby on the bed beside his proud mother, he slipped his finger into the infant's hand.

Instantly the tiny hand closed on the finger, and held on.

Such a simple thing! Yet for Phyllis how sweet! It conveyed such a tremendous message!

Yes! It was true. This child was normal. Ordinary. Just like the others all around. It was great! Their fears had been groundless and the doctors had been right. It hadn't happened again.

When Hertford returned to his wife's bedside to speak to Phyllis, and gaze in admiration at his second infant son, they decided he should be called Ford. This had been predetermined for months. It just required the rubber stamp of mutual approval, now their baby had arrived safely.

A few hours later Hertford decided he should probably make for home. As he rose to go he said to Phyllis, "I will tell my Da this one's normal, and called after him."

He had crossed the ward, but before he could finally drag himself away he turned back and looked down at little Ford.

"I wonder if this fellow will be able to drive a tractor or clean out a chicken house?" he mused.

Hertford was seeing one of his aspirations realised. He now had a son and heir of the kind he had always imagined.

Chapter 7

'HEAVEN'S VERY SPECIAL CHILD'

After Hertford had gone, Phyllis sat on the edge of the bed, taking a leisurely look around her little private ward, savouring her surroundings. Sleeping in the cot beside her was baby Ford. On top of the locker was a pair of ornamental blue boots with yellow crocuses growing in them. Hertford had been out to do some shopping, after he had seen his newborn son!

As the news of this second child for Hertford and Phyllis began to filter through the Arnold and Blakely network, the bouquets began to arrive. Flowers seemed to grace every useable space.

When the door was knocked, Phyllis called "Come in!" cheerily, expecting to see another orderly arrive into the ward with yet another bunch of carnations or chrysanthemums.

She was mildly surprised, then, to see the door edged open very gingerly, tentatively.

A nurse who Phyllis didn't recognise slipped into the ward. "Hello, Mrs. Arnold," the visitor began. "You probably don't know me, but I know you. May I come in a minute?"

"Certainly, come on in!" Phyllis replied warmly. She would welcome the opportunity to speak to someone. She was in the mood for a chat and usually found it more satisfying to talk to a person than a vase of flowers.

"I have seen you coming and going to physiotherapy with Thomas over this last year," the caller explained. "I am just up here to congratulate you on having another little boy. It is great to hear that everything is OK too. I am delighted for you."

Phyllis warmed to this kind nurse right away. And the kind nurse knew what to do next.

Leaning over the cot, she admired baby Ford. After she had gone through the whole range of 'weight-at-birth' type questions, she launched straight into the 'who-do-you-think-he-is-like?' routine. It was typical mother stuff.

In the course of conversation Phyllis learnt that her newly-found friend had two children, one of whom was handicapped. The other was a normal, healthy, active child. That rang a bell with Phyllis. Wasn't that her family situation now as well?

As she rose to go the nurse said quietly, "Phyllis, I have a poem here that has been a great help to me. I would like you to read it sometime at your leisure. Perhaps it will help you to understand about Thomas. Understand, I mean, that he is a very special child. And indeed you could discover you and your husband are very privileged people too, God has chosen you for a specific purpose. To care for His very special child. I think this poem will make that plain."

Phyllis was intrigued. "What's the poem called?" she enquired.

"It is called, 'Heaven's Very Special Child,' the nurse replied, as she offered the young mother a sheet of folded paper.

"Thanks very much, I will read it right now," was the eager response.

As Phyllis began unfolding the paper, her visitor walked slowly towards the door. "I have stayed long enough," she remarked. "I will go and leave you in peace, Phyllis." And with that she disappeared, just as gracefully as she had come.

Phyllis swung her legs up onto the bed, then she propped herself up with the pillows.

Whatever this poem was about it must be very important. A nurse had considered it worthwhile to seek her out and present it to her. She was determined, therefore, that she was going to enjoy it.

When she had made herself comfortable, opened out and then flattened out the piece of paper she had been given, this is what she read,

'Heaven's Very Special Child'

A meeting was held quite far from earth,
"It's time again for another birth,"
Said the angels to the Lord above,
"This Special Child will need much love.

His progress may seem very slow,
Accomplishments he may not show.
And he'll require much extra care,
From the folks he meets down there.

He may not run, or laugh or play,
His thoughts may seem quite far away,
In many ways he won't adapt,
And he'll be known as 'handicapped.'

So let's be careful where he's sent,
We want his life to be content.
Please Lord find the parents who
Will do this special job for You.

They will not realise right away,
This lending role they're asked to play.
But with this child sent from above,
Comes stronger faith and richer love.

And soon they'll know the privilege given,
In caring for this child from heaven.
Their precious son so meek and mild,
Is 'Heaven's Very Special Child.'"

Having read the poem through once, Phyllis felt compelled to read it again. Then again. And again. It gripped her. It transfixed her.

After the fourth or fifth reading a strange sensation came over her. It was as though time had put on its brakes. It felt as if she was being suspended somewhere between heaven and earth.

It was an awesome, yet unbelievably reassuring, sense of God.

April sunlight streamed in through the window. The clusters of flowers stood about like guardians of the heavenly realms. Colourful celestial custodians.

Baby Ford snuffled and wriggled occasionally.

Many of the lines she had read struck home to the mother's heart.

'He may not run, or laugh or play.' It had been some experience grappling with that realisation.

'And he'll be known as 'handicapped.'' There was that word again. Hertford and she had spent many agonising months learning to entertain that word in their thoughts not to mention speaking it from their lips.

It seemed so harsh. So real, so cold, when you saw it in print.

'Handicapped!'

The underlying message of the poem was what mattered, however, and it was different. It shed a new light into an old gloom.

'Please Lord find the parents who
Will do this special job for you.'

Were Hertford and she really THAT 'special?' Could they be, actually, 'special' to God?

Well, yes. They had been giving little Thomas 'the much extra care' he required. They had their feet on rung number one on God's ladder of 'Special.'

They had also been able to come to terms with the recognition that 'in many ways' Thomas wouldn't 'adapt.' It had taken some time but they got there. Eventually.

Now they were two steps up, and climbing.

Had they not developed a much richer bond of love as a result of their shared experiences in that first year with Thomas?

Of course they had.

Phyllis was beginning to feel good about all this. She was starting to congratulate herself. Feel smug, almost. When she reflected on this poem she could identify at least three ways in which her family was special to God.

This made it three rungs up the ladder. And still climbing.

Then came the shock.

When Phyllis reached forward to put her foot on the next step of this imaginary ladder to God, which she was mounting with growing enthusiasm, it wasn't there!

There was a rung missing! There was a great gaping hole where the next step should have been!

She was on the ladder of Special.

She was up the ladder of Special.

She was STUCK on the ladder of Special.

What about the 'stronger faith?'

The challenge penetrated like a fiery dart into her self-congratulating soul.

'Stronger faith.' Where WAS her faith in God?

Buried. Hidden. Forgotten.

God spoke to Phyllis directly through an awakened conscience in the sunlit solitude of that private ward. In His divine wisdom He had arranged for her to be left undisturbed for twenty minutes, alone with her thoughts. The bouquet-bearers had stopped knocking and her baby was still asleep. His tiny mouth opened in a tiny yawn every so often. All was still.

Phyllis allowed the poem sheet to rest on the bedclothes in front of her. She felt happy and sad, mixed-up and guilty, all at once. As she scrutinised every inch of the body of her infant son, again and again, as he lay there beside her, perfectly healthy and blissfully asleep, she felt grateful to God and ashamed of herself.

She had been wrong to be so harsh. It had been one big mistake to presume that God had been punishing her. 'Heaven's Very Special Child' put a whole new complexion on the situation. It was something she had never even thought about before.

Lying right back on the pillows, Phyllis closed her eyes. As she did so a welling-up tear overflowed down her cheek.

"Lord, forgive me," she prayed, silently, earnestly.

"Forgive me for thinking You were punishing me by giving me Thomas. I see now the reason for it all."

Pausing a moment, she opened her eyes to check on little Ford, then closed them again to continue fervently.

"Lord, I want to come back to You. Help me. Help me, please. I'm so sorry. I have so much to thank You for. Thank you for Hertford. Thank You for Thomas. And thank You for this lovely, normal baby boy."

Her prayer ended with a heartfelt request for divine assistance. She had been away from God for too long. It had been a struggle trying to cope without His power.

"Help me to be strong, Lord," she begged.

"I want to be strong for Hertford.

I need to be strong for Thomas.

I would like to be strong for Ford.

And I would love to be strong for You."

When she reopened her eyes the spring sunlight was still streaming into the ward. The flowers still held their heads up high. Ford was still sound asleep.

Phyllis was aware of a glowing radiance on her cheek.

She was also aware of a growing peace in her heart.

She had started out on the long road back.

Chapter 8
MOVING HOUSE

When Phyllis came home from hospital she was a mother of two. She had two equally loved, but very different, sons.

Summer was approaching and the young parents looked forward to long sunny days with the windows and doors of their little house wide open, and both infant boys lying outside in the garden.

It didn't work out that way.

The summer of 1985 turned out to be one of the wettest for many years. It seemed to rain every single day. Their house began to show signs of damp. Phyllis became uneasy. She couldn't ever seem to get it dried out.

One thing that didn't worry her, though, was feeding Ford in the night. A few minutes at the Aga heated the bottle, Ford downed it in ten minutes, and everyone was back to sleep again! Great!

The wet summer progressed into a wet autumn.

The barley crop was lost. Flattened by rain and soaking wet it couldn't be saved. Ford senior, Hertford's father, bought some sheep to put into it. They could either eat it up or tramp it down, leaving the fields ready for ploughing again.

It was a major problem for Ford the father and Hertford the son. Ford the grandson wasn't too bothered about the barley. Not yet, anyway.

The continuing wet weather brought with it continuing and somewhat worsening dampness in the young couple's home.

Phyllis was concerned about Thomas. He seemed to develop colds very easily. At times she worried about his health. She was convinced that the damp conditions in which they were living were contributing, at least in some way, to her 'very special child's' frequent colds.

One day when Mrs. Arnold called to see Phyllis and the boys, and help where necessary, Phyllis voiced her concerns to her mother-in-law.

"I'm a bit worried about Thomas," she began.

"What do you mean 'worried' about him? In what way?" Jean Arnold was only mildly concerned. She was sitting looking at Thomas and he seemed to be perfectly OK.

"It's nothing serious," Phyllis reassured her. "It's just that with this house being so damp and the winter coming on, I'm afraid that these colds Thomas keeps catching will get worse. All this damp just can't be good for him. You know what I mean?"

Jean did understand her daughter-in-law's deep disquiet. And she was so practical. If there was a sensible solution to an everyday problem, Jean would find it.

"Well I tell you what to do," she suggested. "Why don't the four of you move up with us for the winter at least? We have spare bedrooms now you know!"

That was the answer. Phyllis didn't need a lot of persuasion!

Thus it was that in October 1985, Hertford, Phyllis, Thomas and Ford moved in to share the Arnold family home. Initially, it was their intention to winter there.

There was no big flit. The grateful parents just carried the most urgently needed of their bits and pieces across the yard, as and when they were required.

It proved to be a prudent move. Hertford and Phyllis now had a large en-suite bedroom. Everywhere was carpeted. There were no freezing feet on terrazzo floors in the middle of the night here. No standing with one foot in the oven!

Thomas and Ford had their own bedroom. It was ideal for them, a big bedroom with dry walls. Their caring mum and dad repapered it for them, and the paper actually stuck to the walls! They did it with nursery paper – all kittens and balloons, rainbows and clouds. There was a white carpet on the floor.

Hertford and Phyllis were determined to spare neither time, effort nor expense making that room as cosy as possible for their two little sons. Everything had to be of the best!

Moving up to the 'big house' reminded Phyllis of her Blakely days. She liked going upstairs to bed. They had space to spread themselves now, in this larger house.

A family friend made a special playpen for Thomas. Since he was a big child for his age, but unable to stand up, it had to be more spacious than normal. This almost two metres square playpen sat in the middle of the floor in a large downstairs room. Thomas lay in it quite contentedly, rolling over now and again when he felt like it.

Life soon settled into a new routine for the family of four. They were all happy in these more spacious and healthy surroundings.

Phyllis still had to take Thomas for his hospital appointments. Then there were the exercise sessions and longer feeding periods.

Since she was compelled to spend so much time attending to Thomas and his ongoing needs, Phyllis had less time than she would have liked to devote to her younger son, Ford.

That is where her mother-in-law proved to be such a tremendous help. She played the role of mother to Ford. While Phyllis was caring for Thomas, whether nursing, feeding or changing, 'Granny Jean,' as she had become affectionately known, was doing the same for Ford.

As Christmas approached, Hertford and Phyllis had to do some shopping. They had more enthusiasm for it this year. They felt privileged to have two sons, with their different needs, to cater for.

For Thomas they bought the usual array of rattles and cuddly, squeaky and musical toys. The collection was much the same as the previous year, really.

But for Ford they had different ideas. He was going to be a farmer wasn't he? Just like Granda Ford and his daddy.

So they bought him a tractor, a big blue one with a red trailer. They had to give their boy the right ideas. Start him off with a set of farmyard wheels!

Not as one of his Christmas presents, but as something they were convinced he needed, they bought Ford a 'walkie-pen.'

When they put him into at first he just hung there, gazing round him. Then he discovered that if he moved his feet this thing moved as well! In just a few days he was zooming into every corner of the downstairs of the house.

As Thomas lay in his play pen, listening to his musical toys, Ford was often making a circuit of it as part of yet another journey of discovery. He soon found that the family table was high enough to allow him to duck down, get underneath it and come out the other side. He really loved that, doing it over and over again to the amusement of all!

Christmas, 1985, was so exciting for Hertford and Phyllis. Now they had two children with whom to share it as well as mum and dad Arnold, their kind and patient hosts.

Phyllis so enjoyed wrapping the presents that Christmas Eve. It reminded her, too, of childhood days in the Blakely home, when she used to 'hang up her stocking.' There was that same excitement, that same sense of anticipation.

Only now the satisfaction would be in observing the

pleasure of Thomas with his presents, and the excitement of Ford when receiving his.

She wasn't disappointed. For her, and her husband, and for them all as a family, that Christmas was a most memorable occasion. The deep sense of togetherness felt that day was evident in a simple situation which arose.

The sturdy box in which the big blue tractor had come lay abandoned in the middle of the living-room floor. Some roughly-torn Christmas paper still clung valiantly to its side. It was surrounded by all the Christmas fripperies that make the festive season so special. Bows, tags, coloured ribbons.

Someone lifted Thomas and set him gently into the large box, taking care to prop him up in the corner. Noticing that there was still some space left in the corner diagonally opposite, someone else lifted Ford and placed him in it.

Phyllis rushed for the camera. She wanted to record the moment. As she put the viewfinder up to her eye she felt complete, somehow.

There was a certain sense in which she knew she had 'arrived.'

At least one of their dreams had come true. Thomas had company, and it was tailor-made for him.

It was his own little brother!

Chapter 9
FIRST STEPS

With Christmas over, the New Year had begun. And what a start! Phyllis discovered she was expecting a third baby.

She and Hertford weren't concerned about this at all, however. In fact, they were extremely pleased. Thomas was progressing, slowly but surely, within the limits of what he would ever be able to achieve, and Ford was growing normally. It was an absorbing exercise for the young parents, to compare his development with that of Thomas, at the various ages and stages.

A third child would fill another chair around the big table eventually, no doubt. Their family dream was being realised, as fast, if not faster, than they had ever dared to imagine. The terrific plus point about having a third member in their family was that he or she would be an able and active playmate for Ford.

Wasn't the possibility of their having another handicapped child just 'one in a million?'

It would be great to have them all so close, too, they reckoned. This meant they would grow up together and be company for one another. Marvellous.

In late May, 1986, they embarked upon something Hertford and Phyllis had always dreamed of. Something they used to talk about by the fireside on long, dark, stormy winter evenings.

It was a family holiday. Just the four of them together with lots of precious time to spend with Thomas and Ford.

In order to allow them to cater for their children's specific individual needs they arranged to go for a week to Phyllis's father's caravan in Castlerock.

How they looked forward to it! Talked about it! Planned it!

When the big day came, and they arrived at the caravan which was to double as the family home for the next week, it was raining. This was nothing new for Northern Ireland, but likewise not ideal for the start of a caravan holiday. Sitting in the car they decided on their plan of action.

"You stay in the car with the boys, Hertford," Phyllis suggested to her husband. "I'll get into the 'van and check that everything is OK. Then you can bring the children in."

With that agreed Phyllis dashed over to the caravan, opened up, and stepped inside. She was met by that furniture-and-fabric fustiness which is a characteristic of closed-up caravans. After opening a few windows, 'to let in a breath of fresh air,' she made a quick inspection to satisfy herself that all was in order. Then she went to the caravan door and signalled to Hertford to bring in the children.

As Ford would be easier to transport, his dad decided to take him in first. Having carried his younger son over to the caravan door, he reached in as far as he could and placed him on the floor. Then he turned away to go back for Thomas.

That was when the unexpected occurred.

Phyllis had been trying to figure out the complexities of getting the table up when she decided to take a glance over to make sure Ford was safe.

Then she just stared. He had pushed himself up on to his feet. There he stood, swaying gently.

Suddenly, deliberately, he started walking towards his mother.

She was awestruck.

By the time Hertford returned to the caravan door with Thomas, Phyllis was hugging Ford warmly.

"Do you know what has just happed there, Hertford?" she began, not sure whether to laugh or cry. Her husband hadn't a clue what had happened, and was totally at a loss to know what to make of the look of delighted consternation on his wife's face.

"Ford has just walked over to me!" she exclaimed, almost triumphantly.

When Thomas had been laid on a couch, Hertford had to witness this latest stage in his son's development himself. Completely ignoring the fact that the luggage was still out in the car, and the car door was lying open in the rain, Hertford placed Ford at the opposite end of the caravan.

Holding out his arms, he made the simple request, "Come to daddy."

Little Ford did just that. Having pushed himself up to a standing position, he paused a moment to establish his balance, then came to daddy! On his own two feet!

What joy! What excitement! Ford looked no end of pleased with himself. He wasn't a baby any more. He was a toddler now!

Phyllis and Hertford were thrilled. This was their second son, but their first to walk.

The remainder of that holiday was spent encouraging Ford to develop confidence in his newly-acquired skill. A change in content of the please-walk-for-us-Ford stimuli emphasised their closeness as a family unit. Simple commands to 'come to mummy' or 'come to daddy' progressed naturally into useful requests like, "Bring over that rattle for Thomas," or "Take that biscuit to Thomas."

While they were overjoyed at the sense of family cooperation Ford's learning to walk had brought, it also highlighted something else for Hertford and Phyllis.

They were inclined to be sorry, but had to be sensible, about it, for it had become an inescapable fact.

The gap between the natural capabilities of their two little sons was widening.

Chapter 10
NOT AGAIN LORD!

In late September 1986, Phyllis was in hospital again, awaiting the birth of their third child.

'Will it be a girl this time?' she mused idly, once or twice. She wasn't really fussed about the gender of her next baby, as long as he or she would be healthy and well.

Lying there in the ward she committed herself to the Lord once more. "Please, Lord, let everything be all right," she prayed. Phyllis felt so confident that her prayer would be answered. So confident indeed, that it was almost one of those 'I know it will be OK but I thought I had better mention it to you anyway, Lord,' kind of prayers.

Thomas was 'one in a million.' So he was going to be the only one of his kind in the family. In the big happy family...

As she drifted back into consciousness after the birth, Phyllis heard a nurse's voice. It seemed to echo from far away. "Wake up now, Mrs. Arnold," the distant voice was saying. "You have another little boy. He has lovely red hair. His daddy will be pleased."

Phyllis heard. Yet what registered in her awakening brain was not what the nurse said. It was what she didn't say.

There was no, 'Normal. Healthy. Fine. OK. All right.' These words had not been used.

A sense of apprehension gripped her. It was an instinctive premonition. A baffling blackness enveloped her soul. All was not well. She just knew it.

As her mind became clearer, she began to ask questions

of the nurses who were busily working away around her. They answered her as best they could, but direct questions received indirect answers.

"Where's Hertford? When can I see my husband?" Phyllis was anxious to know.

"He will be in to see you in a few minutes, Mrs. Arnold. Don't worry yourself now," the nurses tried to reassure her, but to no avail.

There was something wrong with the baby. Phyllis was convinced of that. Some strange maternal instinct had been aroused in her, and she was sure it was right.

Who would be the first to tell her the truth? To come out with it straight?

Meanwhile, Hertford was waiting outside the theatre. Impatiently. Pacing up and down. He was aware of an unusual coming and going. There seemed to be more staff going in than coming out. Last to go in was a specialist whom he recognised.

When a nurse emerged with a tiny bundle wrapped in a blanket, Hertford stepped forward to see what it was.

"You have another little son, Mr. Arnold," she said, forcing a smile which should have come easily. She appeared somewhat concerned.

Hertford caught a glimpse of the top of a baby's head, with its 'lovely red hair.' It was just like his own in colour, but very much finer and there certainly was plenty of it!

"Is he OK?!" was the proud father's only question.

His enquiry was also greeted with an evasive answer. "I am just taking him to have him checked over right now," the nurse replied, before hurrying off up the corridor carrying Hertford's third son out of sight.

A deep disquiet stirred within him. 'That's funny,' he thought as he stood puzzled and motionless in the corridor.

'When Ford was born they came out and told me he was normal. 'Strong as a bull' was the phrase they used.'

He was engrossed in trying to persuade himself that it was 'only routine' when Phyllis was wheeled out of the theatre on her way back to the ward. Hertford was invited to follow.

When Phyllis had been made comfortable back in bed, her husband chatted to her. They tried to talk about their new baby, but both of them found it extremely difficult. A giant cloud hung over them, darkening their way ahead. Any talk there was centred around his 'lovely red hair.'

Hertford realised from the nurse's comment, and countenance, that all was not well. He was trying manfully to hide his misgivings from his wife.

He didn't need to. With uncanny insight she was certain there was something amiss as well. Lying back on the pillows, Phyllis just wept silently. She was weak after the birth, befuddled by the anaesthetic and sick at heart.

About an hour later Tom and Ethel Blakely entered the ward. Phyllis saw them coming. Her mother was carrying a blue toy elephant and a bunch of flowers.

"I believe he is a wee red head," Tom began cheerily.

Phyllis exploded into loud uncontrollable sobs.

Mother placed the stuffed elephant and the bunch of flowers on the bed and slipped an arm round her daughter. "What's wrong, Phyllis? What's wrong?" she enquired, her voice warm with love, urgent with anguish.

"It's the baby!" Phyllis blurted out. "I know, I just KNOW there is something wrong with him."

Tom Blakely kicked the end of the bed in frustration. "No, Phyllis! No!" he almost shouted. "Don't talk nonsense! It can't have happened again! Not again!"

Ethel showed her mother love. "Don't worry about it, Phyllis," she comforted, "Hertford and your daddy will go and find out something from somebody."

Hertford, though, had no desire to find out anything from anybody. He already knew enough. All he wanted to do was get out of that ward as soon as possible.

So he went.

His father-in-law followed, only to stop in the corridor.

When Hertford reached the Baby Unit he was alone. When he saw a lady doctor whom he recognised in there, he went across to her. Not being a man of many words at the best of times, Herford hadn't a lot to say now.

"Well, doctor?" he asked, making a profound enquiry with only two words.

It was enough for the doctor. She understood, and shook her head.

"All is not right, I'm afraid," she replied.

Turning away quickly, Hertford left the Baby Unit. There was nothing left to say. He returned to the ward rather more slowly.

When he approached his wife's bedside she was anxious for news. "Well, what did they say?" Phyllis asked earnestly. "What is he like?"

One of these questions her husband could answer. The other he couldn't. He just couldn't bring himself to tell the truth. The whole truth.

"Oh, he's lovely," he said, with all the enthusiasm he could muster. "You want to see his red hair. They are having a bit of a problem getting him to feed, though, so they are not going to bring him up to you tonight."

"But is he all right? I mean OK. Normal?" Phyllis persisted.

"He certainly looks all right," her husband replied.

That bit was true. He did.

Making the excuse that Phyllis was exhausted and needed to rest, Hertford went home, heavy-hearted. On the next evening, visitors began to gather round the bed, but Phyllis wasn't content.

She wanted to see her third little son, Wendsley, as they had agreed he should be called. Hertford pushed his wife in a wheelchair along the corridor to the Baby Unit, to satisfy that maternal craving to be with her child. All the visitors, who were mostly brothers and sisters of the new mum and dad, straggled along behind in a higgledy-piggledy procession.

The young parents entered the Baby Unit, leaving the other visitors to observe proceedings through a viewing window. It was going to be difficult to have their first together-viewing of their third baby in such circumstances. Especially when what Phyllis suspected, Hertford already knew.

Phyllis sat in the chair and a nurse handed her baby son into her arms. When the tiny red head fell back limply over her arm, she felt the same sensation as she had done with Thomas.

There could be no doubt about it now whatsoever. This baby was definitely handicapped as well.

She just wept. Tears streamed down her face unchecked.

The visitors vanished from the window, treading softly, one by one.

A numbness came over Phyllis. It was that awful sense of living-death again.

When Hertford returned his by-now almost despondent wife to the ward, little was said. This was yet another of those 'what do you say in a fix like this?' situations.

Hertford went home, promising Phyllis he would be back to see her, 'first thing in the morning.'

When he came back, as pledged, the following day, two doctors invited both Phyllis and he down to the Baby Unit. The purpose of this consultation turned out to be mainly to formalise what they already knew intuitively.

This was it officially.

"We thought you ought to know, Mr. and Mrs. Arnold,"

they explained, "that this baby appears to be like Thomas in every way in which we can test him. This is totally contrary to our expectations, but sadly it is a fact."

The doctors went on to assure the totally devastated couple of their support at all times. They also promised them, kindly, that Wendsley would receive the same high level of care that had been afforded to Thomas.

Hertford and Phyllis heard little of it. They both had the same instant reaction.

It was simultaneous. It was sincere. It was sad.

They both felt they must somehow escape from the hospital. And sooner rather than later. They just wanted to be together, the two of them, with their children and their thoughts.

Although what appeared to be emotionally imperative seemed medically inadvisable, the hospital staff allowed Phyllis to go home with Hertford and baby Wendsley.

As they drove home that day they were both in mental torment once more. Now they had three children under four years of age, and two of them were handicapped.

Phyllis was inclined to blame God for punishing her yet again.

'Heaven's Very Special Child' had been acceptable. Once.

She could have believed it. Once.

She had even felt good about it, in a peculiar sort of way. Once.

But surely even God couldn't expect them to take it a second time. Not twice.

Was it not rather unfair of God to expect them to rear *two* of these 'very special' children? What about all the other parents around the countryside? Why not share the 'very special' children out a bit? Let some other couple be 'special parents,' just for a change?

Phyllis sat in the car, staring blankly ahead of her, in bitter silence of soul. She daren't voice her thoughts to her husband.

Hertford was as hard as a stone.

'God. Who is God? What has He got to do with anything?'

That had been his response nearly four years ago.

It would be even worse now.

Chapter 11
THE CHICKEN HOUSE

After the initial shock, the icy bitterness of heart melted away more quickly for Hertford and Phyllis with their third son, than it had done with the first. There were three reasons for this.

Firstly, they 'knew the ropes.' They had experience in working with a disabled child. Having acquired all the skills and processes, and all the special adaptations of feeding and care required, with Thomas, coping with Wendsley was relatively easier.

Then there was the dreaded 'how will we face the people?' fear. The 'what do we say to them?' dilemma.

That was gone. Having been through it once and found the family circle most supportive, and the Great General Public to be sympathetic or at least tolerant, Hertford and Phyllis had no problems in regard to that either.

Thirdly, and importantly, there were Hertford's parents. Coming back, as they did, from hospital to the family home meant that there were two more sets of eyes to watch the boys, two more pairs of hands to help. Jean was marvellous.

Gradually, however, Hertford and Phyllis began to feel that seven of them were too many now, all living under one roof. The three boys were company for each other, it was true, but their mum knew that with two of them being handicapped the place would inevitably become cluttered up with all their special equipment. Special feeding chairs, play pens and exercise mats all took up valuable space.

In addition to that, there was Ford. At the age of 18 months he had now become very independent. He could go to the fridge and get himself a drink, or to a cupboard and help himself to a sweet – or to many another thing besides, as it took his fancy! Phyllis was actually going to learn to appreciate Ford's ability to fetch and carry in the coming days, though, as his two brothers grew older.

The stairs posed another problem. Thomas was eating well at his special diet, and was thriving. This meant he was putting on weight, getting heavier fast. But he was 'dead weight' to carry up and down the stairs.

It was true that Phyllis liked to 'go up the stairs to bed.' She did not, however, fancy having to transport two handicapped boys up and down stairs for the rest of her days. Another consideration.

Then what about Jean and Ford senior? Although they never once complained, in fact they rather appeared to enjoy the company, yet it was their house. Their home. Hertford and Phyllis had plonked themselves, plus three, by invitation, in it. It wasn't fair, they reasoned, and it wouldn't be fair in the future, to expect Hertford's parents to live through the emotional, and indeed physical problems, of their daily routine.

One night as they lay in bed discussing the situation the young couple came up with what to them sounded a sensible solution. They would build their own bungalow. Stairs weren't on. It would have to be a bungalow for the boys.

But the dream answer posed a down-to-earth question.

Money. Which in their case they had not got. At least not enough to fund the building of a bungalow.

There was a practical answer to that question too, they decided at length. A chicken house. They would build and run their own chicken house. That was, of course, provided

Hertford's father would be agreeable. Ford Arnold already had four broiler houses which Hertford helped to manage.

If only he had one! Just one, of his own! Then they could make enough, through time, to be self-sufficient.

That was the plan. They were enthusiastic about it.

A business. Then a bungalow. That was the answer! No doubt about it!

Yet before they could see a brick built, or hear a chicken cheep, there were enquiries to be made, permission to be sought.

Hertford knew how to approach the subject. Like many another young man in life, he considered the best way to obtain anything from his parents was to find his mother on her own sometime, and 'in a good mood.' He would then tactfully raise the issue with her.

His mother was a good thermometer, he always felt. You could usually gauge the family temperature by taking a reading of her reactions.

Thus, late one evening, as he and his mother were sitting chatting by the Aga, Hertford seized his opportunity. Phyllis and the three boys were all in bed, fast asleep, and his father was out in the yard.

"Hi, Ma, Phyllis and I would like to build our own bungalow," he began. "But I'm sure you have a fair idea we haven't the money. We were thinking we could start our own chicken house to make a pound or two. Then if that worked out we could build our own bungalow."

Jean Arnold remained silent, but smiled encouragingly, as Hertford continued, "Do you think Da would agree to all that? Do you think he would give us a site for a bungalow?"

When he had asked the second question, Hertford stopped. He stretched out in the armchair. He had finished. Said his piece. Done his bit.

Never mind Da for the minute, what was Ma going to say about it all?

He needn't have worried. Jean was happy enough.

She had felt for some time that for everybody's sake it would be best for the young family to make it on their own. The scheme Hertford had just outlined so clearly would give them an independent income. They would then soon be in a position to build a home of their own in which to raise their family.

Jean liked the sound of it, and said so. "I think he probably would," she replied. "I will speak to him about it later."

The caring mother and grandmother was as good as her word. So successful had she been in selling the idea to her husband that Hertford could barely wait to tell Phyllis the good news when they retired to their room the next evening.

"Do you know what my Da told me in the yard today?" Hertford was bursting with it. Before even waiting for his wife to reply he went on, "He said he would help us to build and start up our own chicken house. AND that he would give us a site in the corner of the field at the top of the lane to build a bungalow on."

Hertford's parents kept their promise. They encouraged their son and daughter-in-law in every possible way in the building and equipping of their chicken house. This was stage number one of their scheme.

On 1st December, 1986, the first day-old chicks were delivered to the house. There were 20,000 of them! They just appeared like fluffy heaving masses as they clustered around the heaters, chirping away.

The clean smell of the fresh shavings and the continual cheeping of the birds gave Hertford and Phyllis a great sense of satisfaction. This was their first independent business venture. They hoped it would be successful.

December brought a further milestone in the life of the family. Another Christmas! What a thrill it was that year!

Now that Hertford and Phyllis had embarked on the chicken house project they had been forced to think outside themselves, and had come to terms, fully, with their family circumstances.

Wendsley was as precious now as their other two sons.

Three boys! More toys! Much noise!

Fantastic.

Hertford and Phyllis, Ford and Jean had a busy but rewarding Christmas. They all realised that if the business-to-bungalow enterprise worked out as they had planned they might not be living under the same roof next December. Everyone had mixed feelings about that.

In late January 1987 the initial crop of chickens was sold out of the chicken house. This was encouraging. It was their first financial return. So far, so good.

Then on 13th February, Hertford and Phyllis watched with their two older sons, as another memorable event, for them, took place.

The diggers moved in to clear and level the site for their new bungalow.

Things were looking up.

Well done to the chicken house!

And the next batch of chickens was due any day!

Chapter 12
BLEEPERS, BUGGIES AND BUILDERS

'Beep! Beep! Beep!'

The big yellow bus from the Education and Library Board was by now coming each weekday morning to take Thomas to school. He had been enrolled in a Special Care School in Lurgan and became so excited when he heard the bleeper sounding.

Arms and legs were waved in enthusiasm, but in no particular order, when the bus began to reverse up the farmyard, right to the back door.

His daily attendance at school proved to be a double benefit to Phyllis. It gave her more time to concentrate on Ford and Wendsley during the day. At the same time it was comforting to realise that Thomas was under the supervision of experts who were trained to care for both his physical and educational needs.

From the time the walls of their new bungalow-to-be began to rise slowly out of the muddy ground, Phyllis liked to make a daily visit to the site.

It was lovely on a spring morning. The daffodils along the lane were in full bloom again and the birds sang and built their nests. The increasing warmth of the sun, when it shone, and the gradual growth of a new home for the family, brought an increased optimism to the young wife and mother.

Winter was over once more. A sense that things weren't that bad after all swathed her soul. On fine days, with Thomas at school and Hertford at work on the farm or in the chicken house, Phyllis would make a pilgrimage to the building site.

Such journeys required much effort. She set off from the farmhouse, the two younger boys with her, one before and one behind.

Wendsley sat in the double buggy, specially bought for Thomas and him. There were two big problems with pushing that buggy.

Number one was the roughness of the lane. Potholes, centre-grass and large jagged stones didn't make for easy buggy-pushing.

The second problem was the design of the buggy itself. Particularly the wheels. They were of the 'supermarket-trolley' variety. All four of them walloped about independently, each one seeming to want to go in a direction of its own. The trouble was not a single one of them appeared to have the slightest inclination whatsoever to go the same way as Phyllis!

Not only did Phyllis have to push on that lane but she also had to pull as well! Besides grasping the handle of the buggy, her right hand had the end of a rope wound around it. The other end of the rope was attached to a blue ride-on tractor with the name 'Ford' emblazoned along the side of it. Perched astride this 'personalised' tractor was Ford himself, aged two.

Although it required a lot of effort from Phyllis, this arrangement worked very well. Very well, that was, as long as Ford stayed on the tractor!

All it required, though, was for him to spot a bee on a flower or a frog on the lane. Then he was away to investigate. He just hopped off the tractor with no advance warning! Two things could happen as a result of this.

The towline could give a jerk and the tractor fall on its side before slithering to either a dusty or a muddy halt, depending on the type of day it happened to be. That was the preferable option.

The alternative occurred when Phyllis had worked up a bit of speed with her combination. In that case, when Ford skipped off, the tractor came lunging forward and whacked his unsuspecting mother on the back of the legs.

Despite these minor trials, Phyllis made many journeys up that lane that spring. A very pleasant spring then gave way to a hot summer. As the bungalow began to assume the shape of a habitable form of structure, the visits became more frequent.

The thirteenth of July was a holiday. A holiday it seemed for everybody except Hertford and his brother-in-law, Estlin. The pair of them spent that beautiful sunny day climbing ladders, stacking tiles on the roof.

School was finished by now, so all three children watched at various stages during the day as father and uncle toiled away. Up and down. Up and down.

Onto the roof with a pile of tiles. Then down the ladder to wipe the brow and have a drink. Then onto the roof with a pile of tiles...

Hertford and Phyllis, like so many who are eagerly watching a house being built, felt that when the roof was on, the bungalow was nearly finished. It didn't turn out that way. There was a lot of fitting out to be done.

Their small cottage-type home had to have the Arnold trademark. An Aga in the kitchen.

There was one special feature of that bungalow which made it different from all the others of its size and shape in the countryside at the time. It had a ramp at the back door.

In the late summer, and on into autumn, the whole family used to go up the lane to explore the shell of their home-to-be. Hertford and Phyllis moved from room to room, clearing up what they could, and planning what furniture they would have in each room and where it would be placed. These plans sometimes changed about three times a week!

Ford loved the empty echo of the rooms. He often stomped about, making as much noise as possible and laughing heartily. Then he would change the mood and creep around as quietly as he could, hiding from his mum and dad.

Thomas and Wendsley sat side by side in their twin buggy. The cackle of their laughter reverberated round the vacant rooms.

It was great for the family to be so close. Being together. Working together. Laughing together. It was a precious time for all of them.

Fitting out slowed down in the winter months and Hertford concentrated his efforts on the chicken house, which was proving to be a success. It was a profitable concern, making money slowly but steadily, not perhaps as rapidly as Hertford and Phyllis had imagined or would have liked.

The spring of 1988 was spent on the finishing touches. When Phyllis made her trips to the new bungalow it was to work, in earnest. There was brushing up, rubbing down and scrubbing out to be done. There was painting, papering and polishing to be done.

Monday 6th June, 1988, which was moving day, began just like any other term-time weekday. Beep! Beep! up the yard. The bus arrived and took Thomas off to school.

Then the flit began, for real. There was no massive removal van required here. No gang of men. On a farm nobody ever dreamt of employing that kind of service.

The removal vehicle was a tractor and horse box. The removal team consisted of Hertford, his father and his brother Tyrell.

Back and forward, back and forward, up and down the lane they went. Pothole-puddle-water splashed away from the wheels of the tractor and horse box. It was a warm but overcast day. There were occasional heavy showers. The flitting turned out to be a coats on, coats off, trying not to get the stuff wet, kind of an operation.

As the items were carried into the bungalow one by one, Phyllis directed the 'removal men' where to place them.

Wendsley sat in his buggy taking it all in, shaking his rattles, and generally enjoying himself.

Ford spent his time riding up and down the lane with the men on the tractor, then running from room to room in both house and bungalow, getting among everybody's feet. And generally enjoying himself!

Eventually everything was moved in.

Now all it required was for everybody to be moved in.

They weren't going to have long to wait for that either. When Wendsley began to kick and squeal with delight they all knew that time was fast approaching. He had heard the big yellow bus coming. The bleeper was going outside.

Thomas would soon be home.

When Phyllis opened the door to go out she was followed by Ford, who suddenly passed her and dashed forward. He climbed up into the bus and found where Thomas was sitting in his chair. Then he helped the driver to remove the straps holding the chair in place.

When the chair was lowered from the bus, Phyllis pushed her eldest son up the specially designed ramp, and into their new bungalow. Thomas had left for school from his granny's house, and come home to his own.

Now they were complete as a family in their new home. Granda Arnold and Tyrell had left. There remained just the five of them, with their own roof over their heads, at last.

Phyllis sat down in the living room, and surrounded by but briefly ignoring the waiting-to-be-cleared-up-clutter, gathered the three boys around her. Thomas and Wendsley were in their double buggy. She held Ford gently with a restraining arm.

Then she thanked God, audibly, for their new home and for the husband and family she had. "Thank You, Lord," she said, "for this lovely new bungalow. Thank You for Hertford and Thomas, for Ford and Wendsley. Come and share our new home with us. Help us all to be happy here. Thank You again, Lord. Amen."

Hertford saw his wife, with their boys clustered round her, and heard her prayer. He just granted her 'a fool's pardon.' He said nothing, though. Although all this religious stuff never did any good, he reckoned, it couldn't do much harm. How could it?

But it pleased Phyllis. It afforded her a sense of peace. She just had to acknowledge the goodness of her God, who had been so patient with her for so long.

The ice had melted further. She had taken God under her notice once more.

Phyllis was on her way back.

Yet again.

Chapter 13
WORK, WHISTLE AND WORK

The summer of 1988 saw the Arnold family settle happily into their new bungalow.

When the school holidays arrived, Phyllis often took the three boys round to her parents' home. Nana and Papa Blakely loved to see their grandchildren.

Hertford was usually hard at work. He had to be, but he liked to be. He had no choice, but he didn't care. It gave him a sense of satisfaction to provide for his family.

Papa took a particular interest in Thomas. With his grandson sitting beside him in his special chair he would talk to him, laugh with him and generally keep him amused. His most unique achievement, however, and therefore the one which gave him the greatest pleasure, was that he taught Thomas to whistle.

They used to sit side by side for long periods and Papa would whistle a few notes to Thomas who just loved this strange sound, and laughed and gurgled. So Papa repeated the performance.

Then, after a few weeks of whistling enjoyment, Papa was absolutely delighted to see Thomas, who would never be able to speak, try to purse his lips to imitate him.

Fantastic incentive for further effort!

Finally, the big day came! The day when Thomas actually made a noise!

He really startled himself! Thomas was so thrilled when he realised that he could make some sort of a sound he did it over and over again. The more excited he became, though, the less control he had and his attempts ended in little more than soundless sucks and blows.

Gradually, over a number of visits, Papa taught his grandson to control his cheek and mouth movements and the whistling improved. When Papa asked Thomas to show everybody what a clever boy he was and how he could whistle, it was often difficult to determine who was more pleased, Thomas the whistler or Papa the tutor!

September was back to school month.

The big yellow bus with the big noisy bleeper returned to the front of the bungalow for Thomas. Ford started nursery school, and Granda Arnold made it his special responsibility to transport his young namesake there every day.

Phyllis settled into an autumn routine of housework, shopping, and taking Wendsley to his physiotherapy classes in Craigavon Hospital. As for Hertford, he just worked and worked and worked.

Cash flow had become a problem. The main trouble was that there seemed to be more cash flowing out than there was flowing in. Their difficulty was not uncommon for young couples raising young families. It was called, 'making ends meet.'

Two crops of chickens had been sold out of the chicken house that autumn but they hadn't been as profitable as Hertford and Phyllis had planned. They could live off the chicken house. That was for certain.

But they couldn't buy anything extra! No curtains. No carpets. No luxuries.

To augment their income, Hertford took on yet more work. He borrowed his father's power hose and went around local farms hosing down hay sheds, cattle sheds and silos. Anywhere, indeed, where cleaning was needed and money could be made.

Christmas 1988 was a blissful time of being together for them all. They were now in their own home and at their own fireside. They had their own Christmas dinner in the oven of the Aga in the kitchen, and their own Christmas tree in the corner of the living room. It was cosy.

Happy and memorable as it was, the Christmas holiday period for the family had, of necessity, to be short. Hertford couldn't afford to laze around right through into the New Year. There was work to be done. He was back out and on to a bungalow roof, hosing down the tiles, in the chill of 27th December, the day after Boxing Day.

With all his endeavours, on the farm, in the chicken house and with the power hose, the situation began to improve. There was hope on the horizon. Chinks of light were beginning to appear in the financial murk.

Still, there were things Phyllis felt she wanted. There were even things she was convinced they needed. The stark reality was that they simply couldn't afford them, nor would they be able to, for some time to come.

She felt that with Hertford working so hard she should also be doing her bit for the furnishing fund. It would be great if she could somehow pull her weight.

What, though, could a young mother, with three children all under five years of age, and two of them handicapped into the bargain, actually *do*?

Well, what?

Chapter 14
NO TRIFLING MATTER

It was February 1989 and teatime late one afternoon.

Phyllis was spoon-feeding Thomas and Wendsley alternately, as they sat in their high-chairs. The chairs were placed two yards apart, and Phyllis sat between them, feeding the boys from trifles she had bought in Marks and Spencer.

Her two sons absolutely loved these smooth desserts. Their mum appreciated them too for the simple reason that the boys were fond of them, and they didn't have to be mashed, strained or pureed.

Suddenly a thought came to her. It was so obvious she was surprised she hadn't thought of it before. I could make those trifles, she reckoned. No problem. All I would need would be some cake, some fruit, some jelly, some custard... all easily obtained ingredients. I could stop and start when I had the time. It would certainly be simpler than trying to bake stuff in the Aga.

That was it. Trifles! Desserts!

When Hertford came up for his tea about an hour later his wife could scarcely contain herself. She was bubbling over with enthusiasm about this 'great idea,' this 'flash of inspiration,' she had just had.

"I know now what I could do, Hertford," she began eagerly. "To make a little bit of extra money, you know,"

Hertford smiled wryly. He was ever so slightly cynical. He was used to these bright ideas. Phyllis had been going to raise bedding plants one week, fatten turkeys the next week and bake apple tarts the next!

"Well, what is it now?" he asked resignedly, as he sat down at the end of the table.

"I would like to start making trifles, desserts, you know, Hertford, in the house. Thomas and Wendsley love them, we are spending a fortune on them, I could easily make them, and what the boys couldn't eat, I could sell!"

When her husband paused from his eating to comment, it was merely to dismiss the whole idea with a 'we have heard it all before' type of reply.

"Have you no wit, Phyllis?" he enquired, mildly amused to learn of yet another harebrained scheme. None of them ever came to anything.

"Think now. How would you cope with all that?" he went on. "Think of all the stuff you would need. And there are the three boys to be looked after. Wendsley has to be taken to physiotherapy. Don't be daft, Phyllis. Give yourself a break."

A sweeping wave of Hertford's arm across the table accompanied his final pronouncement. With that gesture he consigned the entire pudding project to the mists of oblivion where it would join a dozen or so other nonstarters.

Phyllis wasn't going to be that easily put off. This was a good one. She knew it. Not like the dried flowers or the buns in boxes.

She didn't sleep very soundly that night. There were plans to be made, amounts of ingredients to be calculated, a timetable to be worked out.

Next morning was a school morning. Thomas went off in the big yellow bus and Granda Arnold called to whisk Ford away to nursery school. When she saw Hertford safely dispatched to the chicken house, and Wendsley secured in his buggy, Phyllis got out the Yellow Pages.

Having found the heading she was looking for, 'Packaging materials,' she ran her finger down the list. After biro-marking a few of the most promising looking companies, she started making the calls.

"Hello," she would begin. "I was wondering do you sell those little round plastic containers that would hold small desserts?"

If the answer was 'Yes,' Phyllis's heart skipped a beat and she would continue, "Well, could I buy fifty of them from you?"

It was probably a good job the potential customer couldn't se the face of the potential supplier at the other end of the phone. All she could hear was the voice, which was invariably polite.

"I'm sorry, madam," would come the reply, time and time again, "The minimum quantity we can supply is one thousand."

A thousand! A thousand! 'What on earth would I do with a thousand of those wee tub things?' she asked herself.

After the fourth or fifth phone call she gave up and had a good laugh about it. Phyllis could see the funny side of the whole situation. She could just picture trifles on the kitchen bench, trifles on the kitchen table, trifles on the kitchen windowsill... The twin buggy could become an unapproachable island, marooned in a sea of trifles on the kitchen floor...

There must be another way. There must be somebody who could help her. She wasn't going to give up. Surely not everybody in the whole wide world sold their trifle tubs by the thousand.

Then she remembered. There was a fruit and vegetable shop in Lurgan where she had seen small trifles in plastic pots. Two things she remembered about them. They were decorated with 'hundreds and thousands' and only appeared on Saturday mornings.

Phyllis knew the greengrocer well. She bought her fruit and vegetables from him sometimes. Here was someone whom she was sure could help her, and she reckoned she knew him well enough to solicit his help. It was worth a try.

Sure enough, her next call was to prove more productive. Having explained her need, she found the greengrocer most accommodating. "No trouble at all, Phyllis," he replied. "Come in anytime and I will get you sorted out."

Fired with enthusiasm to see this project 'off the ground' as soon as possible, Phyllis decided to pay him a visit straightaway. There's no time like the present when there is something pressing on hand!

The benevolent vegetable vendor supplied her with ten dozen trifle tubs. Any less, he figured, wouldn't be worth melting a jelly for.

On the way home from Lurgan, with Wendsley in his special car seat, Phyllis stopped at a supermarket. There was shopping to be done. She bought tins of custard, packets of jelly crystals, tins of fruit, packets of trifle sponges and two large cartons of fresh cream.

Now she had both the ingredients and the inspiration. All she needed was the time.

When Hertford came in for his lunch he was thirsty. He nearly always was. Chicken houses were dry stuffy places.

On opening the fridge to help himself to a drink he stepped back in mock amazement. It was a little bit melodramatic, his watching wife thought. "What in the name of the world is all this, Phyllis?" he enquired with a sardonic smile. "Are we having visitors tonight or something? Somebody you haven't told me about perhaps?"

Totally disregarding his comment, and while he unceremoniously rearranged the fridge in search of a drink, the longsuffering Phyllis set about explaining the purpose of it all.

"No, Hertford. You remember I told you that I would like to have a go at making some trifles. Well, what you see in there are the ingredients for them."

After lunch Hertford rose from the table. As he approached the back door he couldn't resist the temptation to poke a bit more fun at his industrious wife. "Make sure you call me when the trifles are ready," he quipped.

Phyllis laughed. "Keep you quiet and get back out into that yard," she retorted.

Her husband took the hint, and disappeared. With Hertford back to his work, Phyllis was now in a position to start hers.

She worked hard.

By the time the bleeper sounded, and Thomas returned, she had the bases for six dozen trifles made, and sitting in orderly rows on a big white tray. She put them into the fridge to set, planning that when tea was over and the boys were in bed, she would complete them.

It didn't work out that way. There just wasn't the time. Not to be deterred , Phyllis rose at 6.00 next morning, put custard and fresh cream on her six dozen trifles, and returned them to the fridge.

When Thomas and Ford had gone off to their different schools, Phyllis strapped Wendsley into his seat in the back of the car. Then she opened the boot.

As she struggled out of the front door with her big flat tray of trifles, all neatly arranged in regimental rows, Hertford came ambling up from the chicken house.

"And where. might I ask, would you be heading to at this hour of the morning?" he enquired.

Phyllis knew that he knew where she was hoping to go, but just in case he should be left in any doubt, she replied, "I am going to see if I can sell these trifles."

"Who are you going to ask? Did you ring some shopkeepers? You are not just going to carry that tray into a supermarket somewhere and shout, "Who will buy my lovely trifles?" are you?" her husband teased.

Hertford was not being very successful at disguising his mixed feelings. He loved his wife. What was more, he admired his wife. He appreciated her capacity for hard work, and understood her reason for doing what she was doing.

He was just afraid she was going to make a real fool of herself.

"No. I didn't ring anybody, but I will sell all these. Every single one of them. You'll see!" his wife responded, with apparent confidence.

She too was engaged in a cover-up job. How she wished that the words of her mouth were echoing the real sentiments of her heart.

But they weren't. Deep down there was this niggling fear.

It was going to take a lot of selling to get rid of six dozen trifles.

And it was going to take a lot of eating to get rid of them if she didn't!

Where could she possibly find anybody wanting to buy 72 homemade trifles?

That was the question.

Chapter 15
SOLD OUT

As Phyllis drove up the lane towards the main road that morning, she prayed.

"Lord, please guide me. Direct me where to go with these trifles. I need to sell them, but I don't know where to start."

Stopping at the end of the lane she was in a quandary. Should she go right, or should she go left. It was hard to be sure.

After a momentary pause Phyllis decided to go round to her parents' house. That would be a good place to begin. If her daddy liked them it would always be a start!

As she drove along she was conscious of Wendsley kicking the back of her seat. He loved the car. The crows of his laughter cheered his mother. It made her feel this was going to be a worthwhile jaunt.

When Phyllis arrived in the farmyard of her parents' home at Gracehall, near Dollingstown, her father and mother were on the go. They were going about their early morning farm duties.

They both approached the car, each from a different angle.

Her mother appeared slightly concerned. "My goodness, Phyllis, you are up early this morning. Is anything wrong? Where are you off to?" Ethel Blakely enquired.

Tom, her father, peered into the back seat. When he had satisfied himself that everything was normal he spoke to Wendsley. "Hello there, my wee son," he began. "Where's your bottle today?"

In addition to having taught Thomas to whistle, the boys' granda derived particular pleasure from another of his achievements. He had taught both Thomas and Wendsley to hold their feeding bottles. This proved to be a great help to their mum, for it meant the boys could take their own drinks. It was no mean feat either, considering the very limited coordination the boys had of their limb movements. It was the fruit of hours of loving and painstaking labour.

Phyllis got out of the car and smiled at them both. "No. There's nothing the matter, don't worry," she was quick to assure them. "I just wanted to show you something." With that she flicked open the boot. There, carefully packed on their big flat tray, were six dozen dainty trifles.

Her parents just gazed in wonder and amazement.

"Where are you going with these, Phyllis? Where did you get them anyway?" her mother asked eventually, after the initial shock had subsided.

"I didn't get them anywhere, mummy," Phyllis replied. "I made them and now I am going to try and sell them. But I wanted daddy and you to be the first to taste them. Away down to the house there and get a couple of spoons would you?"

As Ethel made for the house to fetch the spoons Tom chuckled to himself. "What will you be at next, Phyllis?" he laughed. He had heard Hertford poke gentle fun at some of his daughter's 'get rich quick' ideas, now and then.

When the spoons arrived, Phyllis encouraged her parents to take their pick of the desserts. As they ate, she explained.

"I took a notion to make these trifles for three reasons. Firstly, the boys love them, so I have to buy them. Secondly, I can make them at home in my own time, and then thirdly I hope to sell a few of them to make an extra pound or two. Help us to buy some little extras for the bungalow, if you know what I mean."

By the time Phyllis had finished her explanation, her dad had almost finished his dessert. He scraped and scraped at the bottom of the little plastic tub, in case he would miss some. When he was sure there was absolutely nothing left he placed the spoon in the container and prepared to hand it back to his daughter.

As he did so he pronounced his final verdict. "That was really delicious, Phyllis," he said, heartily.

"Take another one there if you like," Phyllis invited. Her dad didn't need to be told twice. When he had repossessed his spoon he did just that!

When the score in trifles was dad two, mum one, Phyllis prepared to get back into the car and rejoin Wendsley who had been watching the proceedings through the window.

"If you don't sell them, Phyllis, bring them back and I will buy the whole job lot from you," her father promised. His comforting assurance was a measure of both her parents' appreciation of their daughter's handiwork.

Phyllis waved goodbye, and as she drove away consulted her Heavenly Navigator again. "Where now, Lord?" she enquired. "Where next?"

Her Lord was expected to be a signpost. And a leaning post. This was, however, always and only as a last resort and always and only when it suited Phyllis.

On her way back to Donacloney she stopped at three grocery shops. She didn't need to go any further. Her Lord, her Guide, her last ditch Leader, had prepared her customers and directed her car.

In those first three shops, her first three calls, Phyllis sold all 69 remaining trifles.

She drove home with a light heart. Wendsley chortled away in the back seat and she glanced at him every so often in the rear view mirror. He was happy and she was happy. It was great.

But would Hertford be happy? Would he even believe her?

When the car pulled up at the front of the bungalow, Hertford appeared as if from nowhere. He had been secretly, almost anxiously, waiting for her to return.

Trying again to mask his concern with a wisecrack, he asked, "Well, what is it for lunch? Trifles, I suppose."

Phyllis smiled as she helped her husband unbuckle the straps around Wendsley's car seat. "No, Hertford. I'm sorry it won't be trifles today," she replied.

Hertford set off towards the house carrying Wendsley. When she had taken the empty tray out of the boot she followed him in. As he was installing his little son in his high chair in the kitchen, Phyllis rather deliberately propped the tray against a table leg beside him.

Her husband got the message, but he still had to ask the question. "You didn't sell them all did you?" he enquired, almost incredulously.

"Yes, Hertford, I sold every single one of them. Didn't I tell you I would? And what's more I only visited three shops!" Phyllis retorted.

There were two things she purposely omitted to say, though. She didn't dare confess to her mental misgivings prior to her selling expedition, or to the fact that she had prayed to her Lord for guidance. Indeed in all the excitement she had even forgotten to whisper a 'Thank You' to Him.

Over lunch much lively discussion took place. Where Phyllis had been. What people had said. How much the trifles had sold for. These and many other topics were chatted through at length.

Hertford just couldn't hear enough.

Shortly after 2 o'clock when he had returned, rather reluctantly, back out to work, the phone rang.

"Phyllis, is that you?" the voice at the other end of the line had a request. "Could you bring us some more of those wee dessert things tomorrow? We are sold out already!"

"I could certainly," Phyllis was happy to respond. "I will have them with you in the morning."

When Thomas and Ford arrived home from school, the trifle-maker found her husband in the yard. "I have to go to the shops for more stuff, Hertford," she told him. "I will take the boys with me."

Having belted all three of them safely into their individual seats in the car, Phyllis set off. Her mission was to buy yet more jellies, custard, trifle sponges, tinned fruit, fresh cream...

After watching the car speed away up the lane, Hertford decided it was coffee time. He would go into the house and make himself a cup.

While he sat idly by the table, sipping his coffee and staring at the empty tray still propped up at the table leg, the phone rang again. It was five past four.

"Is Phyllis there?" came the query.

"No. I'm sorry she's not," Hertford replied. "She's away out to do some shopping. Can I take a message?"

"Yes. I'm sure you could," the caller continued. "Just ask her to bring us two dozen more of those trifles tomorrow, if she could. They have been very popular today. We are sold out already."

"No problem. That will be OK. I will tell her when she gets back," the once sceptical husband assured the shopkeeper. When they had said their 'Goodbyes,' he replaced the receiver.

Now he was convinced. These trifles were going to take off after all.

The joking was over. He wouldn't, he couldn't, make fun of Phyllis anymore.

She was on to a winner this time!

Chapter 16

DO YOU WANT A JOB?

The end of June brought two added pressures for Phyllis and her trifle tub turnout. They were pleasant problems to have, but required careful planning.

Firstly, Thomas and Ford were commencing their summer holiday from school. All three boys were pleased about that. The two older boys were happy to be at home, and Wendsley was glad of their company.

Then also, with the better weather and glowing word of mouth recommendation, the orders for trifles increased steadily.

To see everything done that had to be done in any one day, a routine had to be established. Those summer mornings began early. When Hertford rose at 6.00 am to make his first visit of the day to the chicken house, Phyllis got up as well and brought the three children down into the living room. One by one she changed, dressed, and fed them. This was a time-consuming operation.

After Ford, who was by then over four years of age, had eaten his breakfast, he became guardian of his brothers, one older, the other younger, than himself.

Phyllis laid Thomas and Wendsley on the living room floor with their bottles, which they had learnt to hold for themselves, thanks to the untiring efforts of Papa Blakely.

As Ford sat on the floor on his knees, watching the early morning children's TV programmes, he would hear a clunk. That was a bottle down. Occasionally, and especially when the bottles were full and heavy, one of the boys would drop his. Thomas and Wendsley could hold their bottles up, but they couldn't pick them up.

Ungrudgingly, Ford would leave off his viewing, retrieve the dropped bottle and replace it in welcoming hands. He would then return to his knees before the TV and resume where he left off.

That was, of course, until the next clunk...

Shortly after 8 o'clock Hertford would arrive in the kitchen for breakfast, and when it was all over and cleared away his wife set to work on the desserts. The utility room now housed two tall white fridges. Phyllis spent the morning preparing the bases for the day's trifles. Sponge, jelly and fruit were all added to the tubs which she had arranged on trays. These were then returned to the fridge to set.

Next was the family lunch break. This was a happy, sharing time. Hertford helped his wife with the boys, playing with them, feeding them and settling them.

With lunch over it was white coat time. Hertford showered, donned a white coat and hat, and helped Phyllis put the finishing touches to the trifles. Custard had to be added. There was cream to be whipped and spread on them. Finally, the decoration had to be done.

Before delivery, the lids were put in place. The original Phyllis trifles didn't have lids, but now that she was confident enough to order her tubs by the thousand, she was supplied with see-through lids as well! And they even stretched to labels!

August was progressing, business was buzzing, the green blackberries had started to turn red on the lane and every draper's shop in Lurgan had a 'Back to School' poster in the window, when the phone rang one afternoon.

Phyllis was out. Hertford answered.

He was pleased with the call. He was sure Phyllis would be too. It could be their big break.

Hertford thought his wife was never going to come home. He was growing more impatient with every passing minute for he so much wanted to see her face when he told her the news.

She wasn't long into the house until her husband told her about the telephone conversation of an hour or so earlier.

"There was a man rang there a while ago," he began, trying to hide his own excitement behind a matter of fact voice. "A distributor he calls himself. He has what he describes as 'a chilled run.' That means he supplies small shops and service stations and places like that with chilled goods. He has obviously seen our stuff out there somewhere for he wants to know if we could supply him."

Phyllis stopped dead in the middle of her back home again rush around. "I don't believe you!" she exclaimed. She was used to Hertford and his antics. She was sure he was winding her up. April Fool could come in August with him, no problem.

"OK. So you don't believe me," Hertford continued. "I was pretty sure you wouldn't anyway. Well just to prove it's right, there's his number. He is waiting for you to ring him up, so go on. Do it!"

Having been convinced by the number scrawled on the back of an envelope, Phyllis took up the invitation, which sounded more like a challenge.

She rang him up.

It was genuine! She heard the same request Hertford had heard just a little over an hour before. "I have seen your wee desserts, Mrs. Arnold," the caller explained. "I like the look of them. Well made and tastefully presented. I think they would be good sellers. Would there be any chance I could come round to see you later on tonight? Say about 9 o'clock or so?"

Phyllis did a spot of quick thinking.

Chickens, changing, feeding, bottles, bedtime.

9 o'clock. They could just about make it.

"Yes. That will be fine. Nine o'clock would probably suit us well," she agreed. Then she replaced the receiver and flew into a flat spin!

When the businessman arrived, a few minutes after 9 o'clock, there wasn't a bottle, a nappy, a rattle or a squeaky toy in sight! They couldn't afford to give the man the wrong impression. He might think they couldn't cope with his order!

In general conversation, after the usual weather-type openers, the prospective customer asked a number of questions. He was curious about this apparently very efficient outfit.

"Why did you think of doing desserts?" he wanted to know. That, and the next few like, "How did you start up?" and, "Who all do you supply?" were easy. Hertford and Phyllis were pleased to present him with the information he wanted.

The big one soon followed. It was the one they had been waiting for. "Would you supply me?" the chilled-run man enquired.

"Well how many would you be talking about?" Phyllis was anxious to know. It would be important to find out what the phrase 'supply me,' actually entailed.

"I would need twenty dozen a night, for four nights of the week," came the immediate response. The distributor had done his homework. He knew exactly how many he needed.

Phyllis swallowed hard. 20 dozen a night, four nights a week. Hertford and she were at that time producing 30 dozen trifles a week to 13 different outlets. They were finding that workload tough, the schedule tight.

Now here was a man, sitting at their table asking for 80 dozen trifles a week for himself! One customer. One outlet.

Nearly three times their total production level.

30 dozen for their present customers. 80 dozen for this new one.

That made 110 dozen trifles in a week. And that was well over a thousand.

No funny fantasies here. This was for real!

While Phyllis was juggling with her mental arithmetic she was acutely aware of her husband's unease. Hertford was running his fingers through his hair, rolling his eyes and shuffling uncomfortably.

Their eyes met across the table.

Before Hertford could open his mouth to say, "There's no way, boy, we could do the like of that," he had sustained a hearty kick on the shin!

Phyllis had the situation under control. "That will be all right," she assured the customer-to-be. "We can manage that OK."

"Mind you I don't want to be let down." The businessman seemed a little concerned. "I can't afford to be let down," he went on. He was probably worried that he was expecting far more than this hard working couple in their lovely new bungalow could cope with.

"Don't you worry," Phyllis declared confidently. "If we take it on, and we will, then we won't let you down. We have been thinking seriously for some time that we need to recruit a bit of extra help. Your order has confirmed that for us. We will have to do something about it soon."

This disclosure came as news to Hertford. He hadn't realised he had 'been thinking seriously for some time' about taking on somebody to work for them, but he didn't dare open his eyes wide in amazement. And he certainly knew not to say anything. The thought of a second black and blue shin put that notion straight out of his head!

The chilled food vendor went away satisfied, but he had hardly reached the end of the lane before Hertford and Phyllis had begun radically revising their daily routine.

The last week of August was to be the first week of the new orders and it turned out to be chaotic. Totally crazy.

Hertford and Phyllis were flopping into bed late and crawling out of it again early. They had to honour all their commitments and they had pledged not to let their newest customer down. They didn't either, not even once.

The trifles were taking their toll, though. In time. And in temper.

There was only a certain amount of this that any human being could stick.

The return of Thomas and Ford to school in September eased the pressure a little. Phyllis worked all morning in the utility room with Wendsley sitting in his buggy tilted into a backward position in the doorway. He just loved to watch all that was going on. His mum was keen to make sure he felt part of it. She would chat away to him as she worked, and he would respond with contented gurgles. Then, in the late morning, he would fall asleep and doze until lunchtime.

Meanwhile Hertford was rushing through his farm work so he could return to the bungalow as soon as possible. When he was duly washed and changed he busied himself with the trifle order output as well.

They couldn't go on working this hard, and they knew it. Something would have to happen, or something was going to give. It just couldn't continue at this level of commitment.

On a Wednesday morning in September, Phyllis had a telephone call from her sister. The conversation had barely begun when Phyllis felt the pressing need for it to end. "Look, Heather, I hate to say this to you, but I am very sorry I haven't got time to talk to you now," she began. "I am up to my eyes here. There's jelly and fruit all over the place. I will give you a ring later on in the day. It will probably be this evening some time before I get a minute."

Life for her sister was far from busy, however. She had just rung up for a chat, hoping to pass half-an-hour of the morning.

"It's well for you, Phyllis," Heather replied, immediately and honestly. "You are lucky to be so busy. The two children are back at school, I have all the housework done and I am bored stiff. And it's still only a quarter-past-eleven in the morning."

Suddenly Phyllis had another brainwave.

"I tell you what, Heather," she suggested. "Why don't you put on your hat and coat and come round here. I will give you something to occupy your mind. I guarantee I can stop you thinking the time long."

Heather was delighted and went round to the busy bungalow straightaway.

Then she came the next morning at 9.30 am after she had seen the children off to school, and left again at 2.30 pm to collect them and take them home.

She did the same on Friday.

Heather's assistance proved to be invaluable. She was keen, learnt quickly, and had the added advantage of knowing the family circumstances. With her around, Phyllis felt free to take Wendsley to physiotherapy or go into Lurgan to shop.

Hertford and Phyllis appreciated her help and presence so much that they offered her a job. Heather loved the work, and was pleased to accept, thus becoming the first permanent employee of the expanding trifle-making enterprise.

Chapter 17
DREARY WEATHER. SCARY WORD

It was mid-November now, and dark, damp, foggy weather.

One Saturday afternoon Phyllis noticed that Thomas didn't appear very well. He and Wendsley had always been prone to colds and chest infections, so mum was constantly aware of any change in their eating, sleeping, smiling or whistling pattern.

When afternoon became evening and the dark foggy day became a dark foggy night, Thomas seemed to be worse. Continuous coughing took so much out of him it was painful to watch.

Hertford and Phyllis grew increasingly anxious. If this condition deteriorated any further it would result in Thomas being admitted to hospital. It had done so on a number of previous occasions.

As it was Saturday evening they decided to wait until Sunday morning to see if his condition would improve. They didn't want to trouble the doctor or anyone else unnecessarily.

On Sunday morning there was no doubt about what course of action they should take. Thomas had grown steadily worse through the night. His coughing had turned hard and heavy with his breathing laboured. It was obviously time for the doctor, no question about that.

When he had examined the sick child the doctor recommended that Thomas be admitted to Craigavon Hospital immediately.

Hertford's mother, Jean, took care of Ford and Wendsley while Hertford and Phyllis took Thomas into the hospital. It was always a relief, Phyllis felt, to get him into hospital. This was where he could be best cared for. This was where the experts were.

When Thomas had been settled into bed, Tom and Ethel Blakely came up to visit their little grandson. The grandparents each found something to please them. It was something to take away with them, a straw of hope to which they could cling, if ever so desperately.

"He can't be too bad if he can..."

Nana Blakely was pleased Thomas had drunk a bottle of milk. That could only be a good sign.

Papa was pleased that through his weakness and coughing Thomas had even made an attempt to whistle! When Papa whistled softly to him he made every effort to respond, but it must have been difficult.

Breath was in short supply.

When the grandparents had gone home, just ever so slightly more content, Hertford and Phyllis stayed with Thomas until ten o'clock in the evening. Then they thought it best to go home, for a number of reasons. Jean had been very good at caring for the other two boys, but she couldn't keep them all night. Also, and very importantly, they wanted to spend some time with their two younger sons as well.

That was nothing to how much Ford and Wendsley looked forward to seeing their mum and dad!

Beside the family considerations there was a basic, personal, physical need. Rest and sleep.

Over the past two days they had been anxious and agitated. There hadn't been any time to rest. Now with Hertford and Phyllis consoling themselves Thomas was "in the best possible place" perhaps they could snatch an hour or two's shut-eye.

It didn't work out.

They went to bed but not to sleep. It was so distressing. Thomas was very ill. They both knew it, deep in their hearts. Each had an awful, empty feeling in the pit of the stomach. Closing their eyes didn't help for their brains wouldn't stop. They kept whirling on, throwing up thoughts, worries, ultimate consequences...

Next morning Phyllis left home at seven o'clock to return to Craigavon Hospital. Hertford was left to feed Wendsley and do what he could on the trifle orders.

When she arrived at her sick son's bedside she realised his condition had deteriorated further. Now he just lay there, sleeping all the time.

Phyllis rubbed cream tenderly on his face. Then she combed his hair. She thought he was so lovely. She had done for him what any mother would have done for an ailing child. There was more she would like to do, though.

It would be great to feed him. She would be so relieved if she could only see him eat something.

When a nurse came into the ward she told Phyllis that Thomas wouldn't take his bottle at six o'clock. This was disturbing.

Hadn't her mother been so pleased yesterday because Thomas had been well enough to take it?

"If you bring me a warm bottle and some Weetabix I will try to feed him," the anxious mother volunteered. She relished the prospect of actually DOING something, rather than sitting simply gazing at Thomas, while listening to his laboured breathing.

The nurse duly brought a plate of Weetabix and a warm bottle, as Phyllis had requested, and she tried to feed her precious little boy.

It was a fruitless effort. Thomas just didn't respond, when

his mum, with tears in her eyes and a tremble in her voice, begged, "Come on now, Thomas, son. Here's your breakfast. Take some of it for mummy."

No reaction. Not a movement. Not a flicker.

Nothing. Just continued sleep.

Phyllis felt strange. It was as though her son, to whom she was so close, was now somewhere far away. He appeared to have drifted off into some kind of different, distant realm.

Shortly after ten o'clock the medical staff made a ward round. Phyllis seized the opportunity to speak to one of the doctors, whom she knew. "Doctor, Thomas won't make any attempt to eat or drink for me," she began, trying bravely to hold back the tears. "He is not even interested in me being here. That is very peculiar. He just sleeps and sleeps and sleeps..."

"Mrs. Arnold, Thomas is very sick at the minute," the doctor replied, gently. "He can't keep getting better and coming home. His body is becoming very weak, and every one of those chesty attacks weakens it even more. The little body is just very, very tired."

Phyllis was beginning to get the message. It was filtering through to her brain, bit by bit.

When she had stepped out of that enveloping mist of the early morning and in through the hospital door a few hours earlier, she had been strangely conscious of entering into a mist of a different kind. She had passed through a wet clinging mist that made driving difficult into a weird psychological mist which totally obscured the future.

The mist in her mind was beginning to clear. Now Phyllis didn't want to peer ahead to try and identify the shadowy shapes she could just about glimpse through the gloom.

When the doctor had given her a few moments to come to terms with his first statement, he asked a question. "Tell me, is Hertford coming up today?" he enquired.

"Yes he is," Phyllis replied. "He will be up later on."

"Well, I think you should ring him and ask him to come over here right away." Although spoken with all the tenderness the doctor could show, there was a compelling urgency about the underlying message. "We are going to put a drip up with Thomas for he is starting to dehydrate," he went on. "Then we will be coming shortly to take him for a chest X-ray."

The next stages of her son's treatment, though explained so kindly to Phyllis, were lost on her. She just wanted to find a telephone. She had to speak to her husband.

"Hertford, the doctor says you should come up to the hospital right away," she managed to sob out. "Thomas is very bad."

When Hertford heard that message, he dropped all and drove to the hospital, leaving Heather, his sister-in-law, to sort out dozens of trifles in various stages of preparation and to care for Wendsley.

At a quarter to eleven Thomas's dad arrived in the ward. As he and Phyllis sat at their son's bedside Hertford was very upset. Leaning over the bed every now and again, he would whisper, softly, "Thomas, son, your mummy and daddy are here. Open your eyes. Can you not hear me?"

No response. There was not even the faintest sign of recognition or reaction.

Nothing. Just continued sleep.

After lunchtime the nurses came and wheeled Thomas away for a chest X-ray. Within half-an-hour he was back lying in his bed again, still in a deep sleep.

A short time later a doctor joined them at the bedside. "Could I speak to you both for a minute, Mr. and Mrs. Arnold?" he enquired.

When they had been shown into a little side room the

doctor told them the news. It was the result of the X-ray.

"This is the worst we have ever seen Thomas," he began. "Unfortunately, the X-rays show that both his lungs are clouded over, white with pneumonia."

What a shock! What a knockout blow!

"A chest infection," would have been easy. They had heard that often before, and coped.

But not this. Pneumonia.

To Hertford and Phyllis this meant something different. There was a sickening final ring about it. It was a scary, scary word.

Pneumonia.

Chapter 18
IT WON'T BE LONG NOW

The remainder of that day was spent in a hazy blur of alternating activity and inactivity.

There were times of speaking to doctors, nurses and relatives who came and went noiselessly, like the fog. By contrast, there were moments spent in silent contemplation, sitting beside Thomas, holding his hand, putting cream on his face or combing his hair

The medical staff asked Phyllis and Hertford if they would consider inviting their parents up to see Thomas, since he was so low. They did, and the distressed grandparents came.

Later that evening, a doctor spoke to Jean Arnold, Tom and Ethel Blakely, and Hertford and Phyllis as they sat together in a state of stunned anxiety, in the ward. "We have done all we can for Thomas," he explained, quietly. "And we will continue to do everything possible from now on. Just at this minute though, there is little we can do. The body is very, very weak. His condition is causing us some concern."

Hertford and Phyllis went home at midnight. Papa Blakely insisted he would stay all night and give them a chance to go home for a sleep.

When they arrived home Ford and Wendsley were in bed. The anguished parents went to bed as well, but it wasn't to sleep. How could they?

At six o'clock in the morning on Tuesday 14th November, 1989, Hertford and Phyllis drove back to the hospital yet again, through dense pea-soup fog. Everything seemed to be closing in around them. They relieved Papa Blakely who went off home for a few hours rest.

Thomas still lay there motionless, semi-conscious.

The morning dragged by.

Relatives came and went all morning, on padded pussy-feet, speaking in hushed whispers. It was as though they were afraid to waken Thomas, but how they wished they could.

As Phyllis and Hertford's parents and brothers and sisters, one by one, made their entrance and exit, there was a constant flurry of medical activity. Doctors entered and left the ward. They brought needles, charts and stethoscopes. Nurses changed drip-feed bottles and checked the heart monitor. Thomas had his chest sounded regularly.

Everything possible was being done for him, just as the doctor had promised. It was all go.

Then, just after lunch, and in startling contrast to the frenetic morning build up, the fever of activity ceased. Quietness, stillness, a strange tranquillity fell on the ward.

The two grandmothers made another brief visit, in and out again soundlessly.

They entered clutching damp crumpled handkerchiefs.

They left clutching even damper crumpled handkerchiefs.

At a quarter to four in the afternoon Hertford and Phyllis were alone in the ward with their very sick son. This was unusual since there had been a constant coming and going of relatives all day. The relatives were still around the hospital at various locations, wanting to be close to the situation but finding the silent anxiety of the ward a little bit too close at that time.

Thomas lay motionless on the bed, still in a semi-conscious state. He was perspiring freely. His hair was soaked in sweat. Phyllis leaned over and with a mother's tender touch, dried his hair, face and neck occasionally. His face had become a peculiar grey colour. The line of his lips was barely distinguishable.

The only sound was the regular beat of the heart monitor.

Sister Mavis Brush slipped quietly into the ward. Hertford and Phyllis knew this senior nursing figure and held her in high regard. She had been ever so kind to them on their regular visits to Craigavon Hospital with Thomas and Wendsley.

On entering, Sister Brush kept both hands behind her, holding on to the handle of the door. She seemed almost reluctant to proceed any further into the ward. She had the look of someone who had something to say, but wasn't exactly sure how to say it.

It was obvious she had been weeping.

Having steadied herself by the door for a short time she took a few steps forward towards the bed. She was now close to Thomas and beside his distraught parents.

"I am going off duty now at four o'clock," she said softly. "But I am going home to pray for you both, that God will be with you in what you are about to come through."

She paused for breath. The sister was taking her time, weighing her words carefully, speaking them compassionately.

"Thomas is very low at the moment. We have done everything in our power both physically and medically to keep him here. He is now barely clinging to life, but he is in the hands of the Lord. For some time now I have dreaded this moment..."

There was a second pause, longer this time. Hertford and Phyllis sat gazing at her. They were in a kind of daze, but appreciated her genuine concern. Even Hertford didn't resent the reference to "the hands of the Lord." Here was a woman who felt deeply about what she was saying. He could take it from her. She lived it.

Fumbling in the pocket of her uniform, Mavis Brush

produced a piece of folded paper. "For some weeks now I have had this poem," she explained, still holding the folded paper lightly in her right hand. "I feel led of the Lord to give it to you now."

With that she stepped forward and offered the paper to Phyllis. Sister Brush kissed the broken-hearted mother on the cheek, lovingly and spontaneously, as she reached up to accept it.

"Is there anything, anything at all, I can do for you, Hertford and Phyllis?" she enquired with great tenderness.

"Yes, Mavis, there is something you could do for me," Phyllis replied. "I would love to nurse Thomas again. Would that be possible do you think?"

"No problem. I can sort that out for you OK," the sister assured her.

Then she gave the instructions. "Hertford, could you lift him out of the bed onto Phyllis's knee, after I switch off the monitor? I will wheel the drip trolley round."

When the bleeping of the monitor ceased there was silence. It was a deep, intimate silence. This was tender-together time.

The sister placed a blanket around Thomas's legs as he sat on his mother's knee. He was so pale. His breathing was very laboured.

The little body was worn out. Spent. Exhausted.

It had nothing left to fight back with.

Hertford rhythmically massaged his son's cold feet.

In a final gesture before leaving, Sister Brush put her arms around both of them. She didn't feel the need to say anything more. She was weeping unashamedly now.

After she had been gone about ten minutes, Phyllis interrupted her nursing vigil by asking, more for something to say, than because she really wanted to know, "I wonder what this poem is all about?"

She tried unsuccessfully to shake the page open. Hertford helped flatten it out across her free hand.

Cradling her extremely sick son with one loving arm, Phyllis read the poem silently.

TO ALL PARENTS

"I'll lend you, for a little while, a child of mine," He said,
"For you to love while he shall live, and mourn when he is dead,
It may be six or seven years, or twenty two or three,
But will you, till I call him back, take care of him for Me?
He'll bring his charms to gladden you, and should his stay be brief,
You'll have his lovely memories as solace for your grief.
I cannot promise he will stay, as all from earth return,
But there are lessons taught down there I want this child to learn.
I've looked the wide world over in my search for teachers true,
And from the crowds that throng life's lanes I have selected you.
Now will you give him all your love – not think the labour vain,
Nor hate Me when I come to call to take him back again?"
I fancied that I heard them say, "Dear Lord, Thy will be done,
For all the joy this child shall bring, the risk of grief we'll run.
We'll shower him with tenderness and love him while we may,
And for the happiness we've known, forever grateful stay,
And should the angels call for him much sooner than we planned,
We'll brave the bitter grief that comes, and try to understand."

No wonder Sister Brush had considered it appropriate. No wonder, either that she had waited until now to present it, tearfully, to them.

"Well, what's it about?" Hertford asked. "You surely must have read it all by now."

By way of an answer, Phyllis began reading the poem aloud.

As she struggled to read it out to him the words of the first line seemed to linger with her throughout the whole poem.

"I'll lend you, for a little while..."

"Lend you – lend you, lend you, lend – lend – lend..."

The poem seemed to be all about a loan. A child had been lent. Not given, lent. Phyllis knew from experience that the idea of a loan was that it had to be paid back, somehow, sometime.

They had been privileged to be given Thomas on loan. What joy he had brought.

Now the loan period was over. The repayment date had arrived. God was about to reclaim His precious possession.

This was reality.

Would they be able to "brave the bitter grief that comes?"

Could they, would they, even try to understand?

At half-past four Phyllis thought Thomas was a little bit better. His breathing did not appear so laboured. Tufts of blond spiky hair were sticking out all over his head.

"Could you lift him back into bed again, Hertford?" she asked her husband.

Just as Hertford was straightening the limp, unconscious body of his oldest son in the bed, and Phyllis was smoothing the bedclothes and preparing to comb his hair yet another time, Sister Brush reappeared.

She hadn't gone home, obviously. She had grown to know Thomas and his devoted parents well over the past six years.

How could she possibly go home, have her tea and then watch TV, leaving them in this heart-rending position?

When she had reconnected the heart monitor and checked the drip, the sister sounded the young patient's chest. Hertford was on one side of the bed, Phyllis opposite him on the other.

"It won't be long now," she whispered. "His breathing is becoming very shallow. Hold on to his wee hand Phyllis. Hold on tight."

The parents didn't need to be told what "It" was, that wouldn't be long now. They knew, but just couldn't believe it. Their minds refused to entertain it. Surely this couldn't be happening to them.

Nor did Phyllis need to be told a second time to "hold on to his wee hand."

She did, and she would, for as long as necessary.

Until "It" happened.

They didn't have long to wait, either. Sister Brush had been right.

The darkness of night was beginning to obscure the foggy grey of the foggy day. Street lamps were struggling to stretch piercing fingers of light into the encircling fog.

It was ten to five.

Thomas gave a tiny smile followed by a heavy sigh.

Then he departed for heaven.

There was an uncanny, eerie silence.

The laboured breathing had ceased. The beeping of the monitor had stopped.

So this was death.

This was the final parting, the last instalment, the ultimate repayment.

This was "It."

Suddenly the silence was shattered by a shrill scream.

"Thomas! Thomas! My wee Thomas!"

It was Phyllis. It was a mother's piercing wail.

Hertford and she felt they just wanted to run away, taking their little treasure with them. Could they not whisk him off to some secret hideaway, somewhere they could go to visit him when they wanted, hold him when they liked, forever?

Having allowed the absolutely beside themselves parents a lengthy period of uninterrupted deeply personal grief, Sister Brush appeared again.

When she had sympathised feelingly with Hertford and Phyllis, she began to guide them back towards reality. It was difficult, oh so difficult. Almost impossible.

"Would you like to have him home later on tonight?" she enquired, sensitively.

"Yes, we would. Of course we would." This was the instinctive and understandable response of a grief-stricken mother whose mind was struggling through the mist of a mythical world of disbelief.

Of course they wanted their Thomas home. What else would they want?

"Well then, I'm really awfully sorry but I will have to take him away now. Some preparations have to be made you know," she explained with infinite tenderness,

"We know that. We know," said Hertford. "Go ahead."

Those last two words didn't come easily. They took some strength to say.

Phyllis couldn't say anything now. She was speechless, struck dumb.

Hertford and Phyllis stood, side by side, numb with grief and stunned with shock, watching their Thomas, covered with a sheet, being wheeled away from them, out of the ward and down the corridor.

Tears flowed freely from swollen, reddened eyes.

How could they be expected, ever, ever, ever to understand THIS?

Chapter 19
'SAFE IN THE ARMS OF JESUS'

Hertford and Phyllis drove home from the hospital in absolute silence. They were dazed. Confused. Dumbfounded.

As they approached their bungalow, down the lane, they noticed that all the curtains were drawn. Caring relatives were in before them. They had come to help prepare them for the sense of loss, the tragedy of bereavement.

Approaching the front door, the heart-broken parents were able to see up the hall through the glass panel. Wendsley was lying in the hall, rolling over. They paused, weeping, on the step. How were they going to tell him his older brother, his playmate, wouldn't be coming back? How could they ever get him to understand that he would never become excited again at the sound of the big loud bleeper on the big yellow bus, for it wouldn't be coming back either?

When they managed to compose themselves sufficiently, Hertford and Phyllis stepped inside their home. Although a number of kind and loving relatives were there, waiting to comfort them, they were struck immediately by an impression of emptiness. There was a feeling that something, someone, some vital part, was missing, and it was gone for good.

Things were never going to be the same again.

Unable for the moment to face the assembled well-wishers, Phyllis scooped Wendsley up from the floor and carried him into her bedroom. There she sat with him on her knee, and cried and cried.

How could she ever attempt to explain this to him? Could

she even explain how she felt to anybody, for that matter? It would be impossible.

It brought some sense of comfort to have Wendsley on her knee, hugging him tightly. At least he was still there.

At a quarter-to-nine the undertaker arrived with a little coffin.

Phyllis stayed well out of the way while Hertford and some others removed Wendsley's cot from the boys' bedroom, so Thomas could be left in his own room. Only when all the minor removals were complete did the grief-stricken mother pluck up the strength to venture in.

Thomas was home. That was what she had wanted.

As she sat alone, and devastated, in that room with the body of her little son, Phyllis realised something else.

It was something different, something comforting.

Sitting looking at the wallpaper which she and Hertford chose for their sons' bedroom back in those happy moving-in and decorating days, she remembered a comment she made more than once at the time. "I love the way the clouds and the rainbows are looking down on the boys," she remarked. "This is their own little heaven."

There slowly dawned upon her numbed soul the consciousness of a tremendous and indisputable fact. Thomas was now IN heaven, the real heaven, the heaven of heavens, where God lives.

He was looking down on the clouds and rainbows! Could he be looking down on her too, sitting there alone, overwhelmed by grief?

Thomas was now at home, but it was in his final, eternal, happy home.

Her ever so slightly soothing reverie was interrupted by Hertford entering the room.

"Phyllis, the undertaker would like to speak to us for a few minutes. There are some things he needs to know about what we want put into the paper. Can you face it?" he enquired.

"Oh yes. Don't worry Hertford, I will come," she replied, and followed her husband into the living-room.

Wendsley lay on the floor gazing up at the three adults towering above him, as they began to talk.

"There are just some details I need to know so I can put a notice in the paper," the undertaker explained.

Hertford and Phyllis nodded. They were going to find it tough, but they understood. The man had his job to do.

"There are three main questions," he went on. "Firstly, what was his full name? Then what age was he? And finally, what time do you want the funeral at? I presume you will want it on Thursday."

Hertford took responsibility for supplying all the necessary information. "He was Thomas Jackson Arnold," he said. "He was six years of age. Well, five years and ten months to be exact. And I suppose one o'clock would be a suitable time to have the funeral, if that suits you."

As he noted down the details, and confirmed the time of the funeral on Thursday 16th November, the undertaker was conscious of something tugging at his trouser leg. He looked down.

It was Wendsley, with a tiny handful of trouser leg, holding on tightly.

"What an attractive little boy," he remarked. "He has such a charming smile and what lovely red hair!"

"What lovely red hair!" This observation, made ever so kindly, jolted Phyllis. It took her right back to the night he was born. Wasn't that what the nurse said then? Indeed it was all she had said.

"Believe it or not, Bertie," Hertford disclosed, "but Wendsley is handicapped as well."

"Oh is he? I didn't realise," the undertaker replied, obviously surprised. He could be forgiven for not realising. No one did, unless told, for Wendsley just looked like any other little boy.

Phyllis by now had found her voice. She had regained sufficient composure to allow her to contribute to the conversation. "Wendsley is really going to miss Thomas," she reflected. "They were great playmates. The pair of them spent hours together, just rolling over and over on the floor. He won't know what has happened to him."

Acutely aware of the fact that Phyllis was in a very unstable emotional state, the undertaker prepared to leave. "I must go now and see to these things," he said, moving towards the door. Then, turning as though he suddenly remembered something he should never have forgotten, he asked, "By the way, is there anything else you want me to add to the notice for the paper? I mean a verse from the Bible or something like that."

The question didn't apply to Hertford. He didn't know any verses from the Bible.

Phyllis was the one who knew. She hadn't thought of a suitable verse from the Bible, but there was one title of a hymn she decided she would like. "Could you put in 'Safe in the arms of Jesus'?" she requested.

"No problem," was the immediate response. "That sounds like an appropriate line."

Phyllis thought so too. She was sure Thomas was there. It described precisely the position as it was revealed to her a short time before in silent meditation. Her son was in heaven, 'Safe in the arms of Jesus.'

More relatives began to arrive. In twos and threes they came, all sombrely dressed and full of sympathy for Hertford and Phyllis. They hugged the young couple warmly and expressed their condolences sincerely.

"We are very sorry for what has happened," they whispered. "This is awful. Don't be a bit afraid to let us know if there is anything we can do."

There was genuine heartfelt grief. A real sense of death, and what was even more shocking, the death of a child, hung heavily in rooms where red-eyed relatives spoke only in whispers.

Phyllis was so distressed she felt she wasn't thinking straight. She didn't know her own mind. A mystical recognition of the unreal had returned. When was she going to waken up out of this? Surely this couldn't be anything more than a bad dream, a haunting nightmare? When was she going to come to her senses?

As midnight approached a local doctor arrived to see Phyllis, who was by that time lying on the bed. She was staring at the ceiling in a stupor of grief, too drained, too exhausted, even to cry.

"I'm really sorry about Thomas," the doctor began, with deep feeling. After waiting a moment she went on, "And how are you coping, Mrs. Arnold? Do you want any tablets to calm you down?"

"No. I don't need anything I'm sure," Phyllis replied "I think I will be OK. I am a bit worried about Wendsley, though. He seems to be taking another cold."

"Don't worry about Wendsley," the doctor was reassuring. "I will listen to his chest and get him an antibiotic which will probably clear things up in a few days."

The doctor invited Phyllis to ring her at any time if she needed anything, before leaving the room in search of Wendsley. She found him in the living room with his dad and a few others.

Having given him a thorough examination she returned to the bedroom, to Phyllis. She had an idea. It seemed, to her, a good, sensible idea.

"Mrs. Arnold, I have just sounded Wendsley's chest. He has a slight infection, but nothing to worry about. However, I could have him admitted to Craigavon Hospital, at least until after the funeral," she suggested. "If you would be agreeable to that, then he could be given any treatment he needs, and you could be assured he was being well cared for."

Phyllis agreed this would be a satisfactory solution. Ford was already being looked after by helpful relatives. Now Wendsley would be in good hands as well. It was a prudent plan.

The doctor phoned the hospital there and then to make all the necessary arrangements.

Thus it was that in the early hours of the morning, on Wednesday 15th November, Hertford and his brother-in-law Estlin took Wendsley into Craigavon Hospital. He was wheeled into the same ward out of which Thomas had been wheeled some seven hours before.

It was now the turn of Herford and Estlin to drive home from the hospital in absolute silence. Minds were dumb. Speech was frozen.

Visibility was down to eight to ten yards.

The fog was terrible.

It hadn't lifted.

Precious Memories

Wendsley

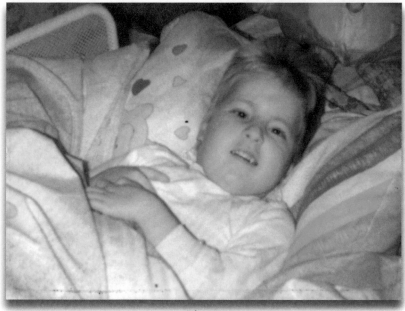

Thomas

Hi boys, what were you at today?

Thomas in hospital

Dad and Ford

...are your feet not cold?

Smile for the camera
Wendsley and Ford

Wendsley

Granny Jean and grandson Ford

Top of the class with Granda and Granny

Lookin good Matthew

Father and Son

Mother and Son

Taxi for Matthew

Ford - strong as a bull!

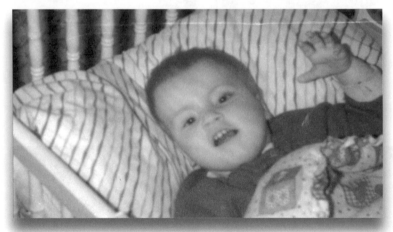

...night night Wendsley

Brotherly love - Ford and Matthew

Thomas and Ford out for a stroll

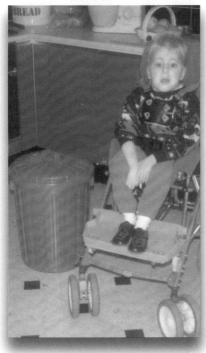

Ready for school

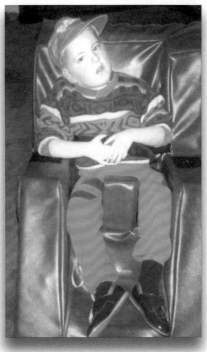

Hard day at school

The three gingers

Matthew - A gift from God

With Granny Jean

Ready for church

Ford, Matthew and Dad

Ford & Matthew -
new set of wheels for Matthew

Granny Jean -
come and get me

Matthew - One year old today

Matthew at
Ballynahinch High School

Just Engaged!

Linden, Estlin, Gloria, Phyllis, Heather, Alva, Jackson
with Mum and Dad

Ford, Nicola and Matthew

Young and in love

Just engaged

Just married

Nicola, welcome to the family

The happy couple

Papa and Nana Blakely

Father and Daughter

Chapter 20
STOP THE CAR! STOP THE CAR!

It was the morning of the funeral. Thursday 16th November. Silent preparations were being made in the hushed house.

Hertford and his brother Tyrell were standing at the back door, having a smoke. They stood on the ramp, backs against the wall. In absolute silence they lit one cigarette after another.

As they stood there, chilled and damp, but glad, nonetheless to be outside, something happened before their eyes. It was something which hadn't happened for weeks.

The fog began to lift.

Big shafts of sunlight broke through the clouds. They lit up the patches of stubble on the field behind the house. Suddenly, for the first time in ages, something had pierced the gloom. A patchwork of light was woven on the field.

The two brothers stood beholding.

"Wouldn't you just think those shafts of sunlight were big ladders coming to take Thomas away up to heaven?" Hertford remarked at length.

That was the whole conversation. It was all that needed to be said. Neither Hertford nor Tyrell spoke again. They just remained, silently weeping, each engrossed in his own thoughts.

When they did eventually re-enter the house, Tyrell rejoined the others who were flitting from the lounge to the kitchen. They were all possessed with that frustrating feeling of wanting to do something but not knowing what to do, wanting to say something but not knowing what to say.

Hertford went into the bedroom where Phyllis was sitting alone. It was where she wanted to be. She couldn't bear to see people and she didn't want to hear people, no matter how kind or caring they were. She had got beyond that.

All she wanted was to be alone. Solitude was sweet.

"At least that old fog is away," Herford said, trying to open a conversation. "It's getting really clear outside."

Phyllis nodded. She couldn't be bothered with conversation, couldn't think of a sensible or significant reply.

Truth to tell she couldn't really care in the slightest what it was like outside. It was probably good the fog had cleared away, but it felt as though she hadn't been out the door for days.

The clock seemed to race along that morning. With the flurry of people coming and going, awaiting the funeral, the morning soon passed.

Much tea was made. Some of it was drunk.

At twelve-fifty the big black hearse drew up at the door. There was a heavy monotonous drone off it.

One o'clock came and the weather had cleared. There was a cloudless sky for the first time in many days.

The crowd was unbelievable. The whole countryside had turned out. People spilled out of the bungalow at both front and back.

The drive was lined. The lane was lined.

Some walked behind the hearse. Some stood and watched, for the lane was so thick with people there wasn't anywhere for them to walk.

Many wept.

The funeral procession walked the mile between the bungalow and the village of Donacloney. There was a simple church service, and then it was off to the cemetery in Dromore.

The winter sun was low in the sky as they drove along.

This created a slowly-moving sombre shadow of the hearse in the hedgerows which had by then changed from summer green through autumn gold to winter bleak.

It was sunset when they left Dromore to come home. Four-thirty. The sun was setting in a ball of fire.

When Hertford and Phyllis arrived back at their bungalow it seemed like there had been an invasion. There were well-meaning people everywhere. The heart-broken couple only stayed half-an-hour.

"Let's go to the hospital and see Wendsley," Phyllis suggested.

"Good idea," agreed Hertford, who was so restless he didn't know what to do. "Come on."

With that they went out into the car and set off. As they were driving between Lurgan and Portadown, roundabout after roundabout, Phyllis looked across at her husband. He was lighting up yet another cigarette.

Suddenly she shouted, "Stop the car! Stop the car!"

Hertford was startled. "What's wrong Phyllis? What's wrong?" he enquired anxiously.

He didn't stop the car, but slowed down to deal with this sudden emergency which seemed to have arisen.

"It's us, Hertford," she began to explain. "It's us. We are not ready to die. If anything happens to you or me we will never see Thomas again. Thomas is in heaven. What has been the point of it all if we are never going to see him again?"

Although not prepared to admit it openly, Hertford had been thinking the very same thing.

"I tell you what we will do," he determined "Hold on until we see Wendsley. Then when we get home we will have somebody round to sort all this out."

Phyllis was satisfied with that. "All this," as he had described it, certainly needed to be "sorted out."

On arriving in the hospital ward they found Wendsley pulling himself up at the bars of his cot. This was something new, something encouraging. Another shaft of sunlight had pierced the surrounding gloom. His despondent parents had never witnessed him make such a sustained effort to pull himself up before.

A doctor joined them in the ward. "Wendsley is ready for home anytime," he told them. "We will keep him here for a few more days, though, to allow you both to settle down after what you have been through. Would you like that?"

"That would be marvellous," Phyllis replied. It sounded a great idea.

As he was leaving them the doctor said, "Just give us a few hours notice when you are ready, and you can have him home."

When the three of them were left together again in the ward, Phyllis and Hertford sat on either side of Wendsley's cot. They watched his every move, helped him when he was struggling and tried bravely to smile back every time he looked up at them.

After a short time Phyllis put her head down on her hand and moaned in misery. "Lord, is this why you gave us two handicapped boys?" she cried aloud in anguish. "So you could take the one and leave the other?"

There seemed to be so many questions, and so few answers.

Chapter 21
THE DREAM OF DEATH

Hertford and Phyllis arrived home later on that Thursday evening. Things were quieter. The crowds had dispersed.

Finally, the last of the close relations bade their tearful farewells,. The grieving parents were left alone. They decided to go to bed early. They were physically exhausted, mentally numb and emotionally upset. Rest was a top priority.

Eventualy, in the small hours of Friday morning, they cried themselves to sleep. Their sleep, however, was not the contented sleep of a tired body. It was the restless sleep of a tormented mind.

In the middle of that night, while in a troubled state of soul, Hertford had a dream.

He saw it all plainly. It was frighteningly real. He felt he was reliving the most unpleasant experience of his life all over again. Moment by moment. Dust to dust. Tear by tear.

In his dream Hertford was back in the cemetery in Dromore. He saw the crowds and felt the chill of the November day. It was strange the way in which the late evening sun lit up the faces of the mourners around the open grave. They all had a pale orange glow.

Looking into the grave he saw the nameplate on the coffin. Thomas Jackson Arnold.

Then came the clods of earth. They clattered and thumped on to it. Gradually, slowly, it was covered...

In this horrible, realistic dream there was a message for him.

The bereaved father felt it. He knew it. He was terrified by it. The message was simple, as clear as day.

Death was coming back.

Hertford awoke, petrified.

He reached over in the bed and shook Phyllis awake. "Wake up! Wake up, Phyllis!" he urged.

"What's wrong with you, Hertford?" she asked, startled to have been so rudely awakened. There they were, relishing their first chance for ages to have an uninterrupted sleep, and her husband was waking her up in the middle of the night!

Hertford switched on the bedside lamp. Covering her eyes from the instant glare, Phyllis looked across at him. She was shocked at what she saw.

Her husband was as white as a sheet. Sweat was sitting in beads on his forehead and running down his temples.

When he saw her looking over he said tersely, "Come on, Phyllis, we will have to get up. Get up there! Quickly!"

"What on earth has got into you, Hertford?" his wife enquired more sympathetically. She could see he was trembling. It helped also when she remembered that less than twelve hours earlier *she* had shouted at *him* to stop the car.

"Death is coming back, Phyllis," Hertford said, obviously terrified. "I know it. I've just had a terrible dream. I saw the funeral, the grave, the coffin, and it's coming back again. The dream made it plain."

"Calm down there, Hertford," his wife advised. She was wide awake now, and realised she would have to settle her husband somehow.

"Don't worry about death now," she went on, soothingly. "Thomas is in heaven, and the doctor says Wendsley is going to be OK. We can bring him home anytime we want."

"You don't understand what I am trying to tell you, Phyllis," her husband replied, frustrated. He was almost frantic by now. "Death is coming back, but it's not Wendsley I'm worried about. It's ME. Death is coming back for ME and I'm not ready!"

Hertford had taken to pacing anxiously up and down the bedroom floor. Phyllis sat on the edge of the bed. She reckoned sleeping was probably finished for the night.

"I am going to have to do something about this!" Hertford was almost shouting in his frenzy. "I am going to have to talk to somebody. There must be somebody, somewhere, who can tell me how to get right with God. I must make my peace with God before I die.

Death is coming back, and it's coming for ME!"

Chapter 22
SAVED!

What remained of that night was spent in earnest discussion.

"Who do I know who could tell me what to do? How do I get ready for heaven when I die for death is definitely coming for me? How can I be sure about it?" These were the questions Hertford asked repeatedly, often audibly, occasionally inwardly.

Finally, after much anguished thought and consideration, the answer came. When it did, Hertford was convinced it was the right one.

There was somebody he knew who would be able to tell him all he wanted to find out so urgently. He was somebody who had made a lasting impression on him as a boy in Secondary School. He was someone for whom he had the greatest respect,

His name was Tom Somerville.

Tom had been his Religious Education teacher some sixteen years earlier. He had also visited Thomas in hospital. Hertford always recognised that there was something different about Tom. He always seemed to have a deep sense of quiet confidence and inner peace.

The man was in touch with God.

Having waited until breakfast time, Hertford could wait no longer. To him, at that moment, getting ready for heaven was the pressing priority. He rang Tom.

Hertford wondered if his former teacher would be

annoyed at him calling so early in the morning.

"I'm glad to hear you, Hertford. I would be happy to hear you anytime," was Tom's reassuring initial reaction to taking the call. "What can I do for you?"

"Well, it's just like this, Tom..." Hertford began, before proceeding to pour out his heart to the understanding and sympathetic listener. He reminded him of Thomas's illness and death. He recounted the dream of the night before, in all its vivid detail. Death, he was convinced, was on his track, and closing in on him fast.

"It is quite obvious to me what is happening here, Hertford. God is trying to speak to you. When can we meet and talk about all this?" Tom replied.

In the course of his explanations Hertford had mentioned the fact that Wendsley was in Craigavon Hospital. Considering that a suitable meeting point they agreed to see each other in the hospital at eleven-thirty that morning.

True to his word, Tom Somerville arrived into the ward to Hertford, Phyllis and little Wendsley at the appointed time. He spoke to the parents graciously, sympathising with them on the death of Thomas. Acutely aware, however, that a busy hospital ward in the middle of a busy morning would not be the most suitable place to hold a conversation about the weighty matters on all of their minds, Tom invited Hertford and Phyllis to come home with him.

"Could you spare a few minutes from Wendsley to come round to my house for a cup of tea and a chat?" he enquired.

The invitation was readily accepted. This was Hertford's big opportunity to do what he had promised twice in the previous twenty-four hours, that he must do soon. He just had to talk to somebody and get all these things sorted out!

They were only in the house a short time when Tom said, "You know, Hertford, Thomas is in heaven."

"I don't need anybody to tell me that, Tom. Where else would he be?" was Hertford's instinctive response.

"You know then, if you ever want to see him again, you will have to be saved." Tom was pursuing the subject.

The anxious, frustrated soul was equally emphatic in his response to this second declaration. "I know that as well," he said. "At least, I know I need something. I'm quite sure I'm not ready for heaven."

"You could get saved here today. Right now, you know," Tom went on.

"Oh, I didn't realise it could be as simple or as quick as that," the former pupil replied. "I thought you had to go to church for a long time, and pay in a pile of money. I thought maybe playing the organ or singing in the choir would help a bit too. Does it not take years before you can really claim you are a Christian?"

This instant salvation, this 'saved right now' idea, was obviously a new one on Hertford.

"Salvation is a gift, not a reward," Tom explained. "You need to realise you are a sinner and need God. You can acknowledge that Jesus died on Calvary to take away your sins and ask Him into your heart. What's more, you can do it this very moment."

This was what Hertford really wanted. It was what he was craving for, to have his sins taken away. Above all, what he most desired was the assurance that he would be in heaven, with Thomas, when death arrived to take him.

There and then Hertford fell to his knees at a chair. Pouring out an agonised soul in stumbling speech, he repented of his sins and asked the Lord Jesus Christ to come into his heart to cleanse him and fit him for heaven.

When Hertford had finished praying he remained kneeling, his face buried in the cushions, Tom rose slowly, reverently, happily, from where he had been kneeling beside his former pupil. It was a tremendous encouragement to him to hear the outpouring of a penitent soul coming to the Saviour.

It was fruit for his labours, an answer to his prayers. As Herford began to rise, pushing himself up slowly, Tom exclaimed, "Praise the Lord, Hertford, you are saved!"

It couldn't have been all that straightforward surely. Hertford was convinced he must have missed out something somewhere.

"Hold on there a minute, Tom," he cautioned. "This must all be a load of nonsense, I have heard nothing. I have seen nothing. I have felt nothing. How could I possibly be saved? I don't feel one bit different."

Tom smiled. He was so wise, so experienced, so patient.

"You are not saved by your feelings, Herford," he counselled. "You are saved by your faith. It is an open heart operation."

Hertford pondered this for a minute or two. It was interesting, but totally at odds with all his preconceived ideas. This was a completely new concept to him.

Then he had another thought..It was related to something he had learnt many years before. One of his earlier brushes with religion had been in school, where he had been taught the Lord's Prayer. In it, he seemed to remember, there was a bit about, 'forgive us our trespasses as we forgive those who trespass against us.'

He voiced an immediate concern.

"Tom, if I'm supposed to be a Christian now," he asked sincerely, "does that mean I should forgive everybody who has done anything against me? Mind you I feel pretty bitter about some of the things that have happened in my life."

"Are you going to let the memory of things that happened,

possibly years ago, spoil your experience of peace with God and your assurance of a home in heaven?" Tom answered one question by asking another.

Hertford realised that he wasn't going to let anything spoil his peace with God, or do him out of his place in heaven. When he came to consider it, the incidents which had galled him for so long seemed to pale into insignificance. The hurts seemed to be miraculously healed.

Then came the marvellous, glorious revelation. He was different after all. He had been saved and was definitely changed!

As the lively conversation on subjects formerly foreign to Hertford, like the "new birth" and "the importance of regular prayer times," continued apace, a fresh desire for an old habit flooded back to confuse him.

His body craved it. Something unexplained within him resisted it.

The craving conquered.

"I'm sorry, Tom," the new convert confessed, ashamedly, "but I am going to have to go outside for a smoke."

"Not at all, Hertford, you don't need to go outside. Sure you can have your smoke in here," Tom replied.

As he drew the cigarette packet from his pocket, Hertford looked, and felt, like a guilty schoolboy. Was he not really supposed to be changed?

"I expect you are going to tell me I have to quit these," he remarked.

"I didn't tell you to quit anything," Tom told him.. "It will come to you. God will take away the desire."

He did, too. Hertford had a smoke that day. He felt he needed it. Gradually, though, the desire to smoke disappeared, just as Tom had predicted. He went from smoking forty a day to none a day in a fortnight, and hasn't smoked since.

Such was the mighty transformation that God worked in his life. He WAS definitely a changed man.

As Hertford, now growing in confidence in his newly-found faith, and a mixed-up, but happy for her husband, Phyllis, prepared to leave Tom's house that day, he restrained them.

"Wait there a wee minute," he said. "I have something I would like to give each of you."

With that he left the room and returned very shortly with a red Gideon New Testament each for Hertford and Phyllis. He had even taken the trouble to write their names on them.

"I have underlined a verse in these New Testaments I am giving you," he said. "And I have put a marker in the place so you can find it easily."

Hertford and Phyllis thanked Tom 'for everything,' but waited until they arrived home before turning to the marked verse in their New Testaments. When they did so, this is what they found;

'For He has rescued us from the dominion of darkness and brought us into the kingdom of the Son He loves, in whom we have redemption, the forgiveness of sins.' (Colossians 1; 13 NIV)

When he read this, Hertford could scarcely believe it. Could this possibly be true? Did it actually refer to him? Was he somewhere in the 'we' and the 'us' of the verse?

Could it be that Hertford Arnold, the scoffer and the sceptic, was now a child of God, a citizen of the kingdom of heaven, redeemed and forgiven?

There were far more blessings to this being saved than he had ever imagined. He was now sure he was saved.

He was delighted about that.

He was sure, as well, that he was going to be in heaven with Christ, and Thomas, when he died.

He was delighted about that too.

Chapter 23
THE WISE SHEPHERD

Immediately after leaving Tom's house, Hertford and Phyllis returned to Craigavon Hospital. Although Hertford was now rejoicing in his newly-found faith and Phyllis, in turn, was happy for him, their hospital days weren't over.

Wendsley was still there, and they wanted to be with him. They considered it most important to be near him, helping and comforting as much as they possibly could.

During the afternoon a doctor came into the ward. "Wendsley is doing well," he informed them. "He is ready for home anytime."

The parents considered this proposition carefully. Although he was probably ready for home they decided that perhaps they weren't ready to have him back so soon.

They were both physically and emotionally drained after the experiences of the previous week. Besides that, the weather was still very cold and foggy, not ideal conditions for a sick child with a weak chest to be outside. Wendsley was going to be with them for a long time to come, so they reckoned it would be advisable to postpone bringing him home for another day or two. He would then be fully recovered and they would be in better spirits to receive him.

When they told the doctor what they had decided he understood. Everyone agreed that Sunday would be a suitable day to have Wendsley home, and this was arranged.

However, when Hertford and Phyllis arrived at the hospital on the Sunday morning to collect their little son they received a terrible shock. Things had changed drastically, and for the worse.

As they entered the ward a doctor met them. He had a sombre look about him.

"I'm sorry," he said, "but I'm afraid Wendsley won't be able to get home today. He has picked up some kind of a virus and has been very sick during the night. This morning he will not eat a thing for us here. We just wouldn't be happy to allow him home, at least for another day or two."

The parents were dumbfounded. They thought that with all they had passed through they would be beyond being stunned. They weren't.

Again came this incredible feeling of disbelief.

"But he was all right last night when we left," Phyllis replied. She was struggling to take it in. "He was smiling and playing like he always did."

"I know that, Mrs. Arnold," the doctor continued, sympathetically. "This has happened so suddenly it has taken everyone by surprise." His countenance matched the conversation. He looked genuinely startled, too.

Hertford and Phyllis spent Sunday and Monday in the hospital. It was distressing to watch the deterioration in Wendsley's condition.

On Tuesday morning his breathing became laboured. He was wheeled away to have a chest X-ray. The parents met the doctor in a side room off the main ward to be given the results in the afternoon. It all seemed so horribly familiar. What were they about to hear?

"The X-rays show that both Wendsley's lungs are clouded over white," the doctor said. "He would appear to have viral pneumonia on both lungs."

There was that dreaded word again. A dazed silence followed the doctor's statement. There was a sense of having seen it all before, of being practically able to predict the next development, possibly even the next word.

Hertford and Phyllis didn't speak. They couldn't, having been rendered speechless once more.

The doctor broke the awkward hush. It was a different doctor, a different room and a different set of X-ray plates, yet what he had to say was almost exactly the same as they had heard about Thomas less than two weeks earlier.

"Wendsley has just deteriorated so fast that we can't believe it," he told them. "Every time I leave the ward and return maybe half-an-hour later he has gone downhill even more. We will continue to do all in our power to keep him here, but he is really now in the hands of God."

Again it was so familiar.

Beyond the touch of tender loving care.

Beyond the scope of medical science.

Into the hands of God.

The hospital vigil continued all through that Tuesday night. Doctors and nurses moved silently to and fro in the ward, checking the monitors, adjusting the drips

Wendsley had lapsed into a semi-conscious state by mid-morning on Wednesday. Phyllis craved seclusion, solitude, isolation. She felt she had to close herself away from all the goings-on in the ward.

So, leaving Hertford sitting with their very sick son, she fell to her knees at the settee in the little room reserved for the relatives of patients. She had spent many hours of heart-searching misery in that room over the previous few days.

Now she was in total desperation.

"Lord, You couldn't take Wendsley on us too! This just can't be real!" The devastated mother had taken to pouring out her pent-up emotions to God once more. "Lord heal him, please! Get him better! Don't let him die! Don't let him die! Please, Lord. Please!"

Rising from that settee, on to legs still shaky from sleepless nights and stressful days, a strange realisation enfolded her. She knew in her breaking heart that God was in control.

Somewhat calmed in her soul, but still dreading the coming hours, perhaps days, Phyllis joined her husband bedside Wendsley's cot.

Shortly after three o'clock that afternoon, the ward door opened. It was Norrie Emerson, a friend, to see them.

"I was working in the yard there after dinner-time," the visitor explained, "and I just couldn't get you out of my mind. I had been praying for you both all morning, and felt compelled to come and see you. I hope you don't mind."

"We don't mind at all," Phyllis replied. "It is very kind of you to take time off your work to come and see us."

Norrie's care and concern for the crushed couple was demonstrated in his next action. Opening up his jacket he produced a piece of folded paper from an inside pocket. "I have a poem here for you," he said. "Read it over a few times when I leave. It will help you both to see a meaning in all of this I'm sure."

When he reached forward and handed the paper to Phyllis her heart skipped a beat. She was conscious of a shake in her outstretched hand.

Another poem! A third one.

The previous two had been given to her, one before, the other after, tragic events in her life. Could this be an omen, a sign of things to come?

Sensing that Phyllis was probably scared, but certainly at least uneasy, Norrie enquired, "Do you mind if I pray with all three of you before I leave?"

"Not at all, please do," Hertford responded immediately. He had a high regard for the out and out sincerity of a busy man who would leave his work in the middle of an afternoon to come and try to comfort them. In addition to that, he had also learnt over the few turbulent days since his conversion, the vital importance of prayer in the Christian life.

When he had prayed with deep feeling, Norrie put his arms around both Hertford and Phyllis. They were all weeping.

Then noiselessly, almost reverently, as he had come, he made his exit from the ward, leaving the heartbroken parents and their very sick son to each other and to God.

Phyllis unfolded the piece of paper. Her husband watched her from across the cot. Blinking away the tears, she read the poem;

The Wise Shepherd

The story is told of a shepherd wise
Who, when the day was done,
Needed to cross a stream to get home.
He led, but the sheep wouldn't come.

So he gently turned to the flock once more
Knowing that this was the best
He stopped and lifted the tiniest lamb,
Holding it safe on his breast

While he waded the troublesome stream again
In the light of the setting sun.
This time there was no hesitation at all
For they followed him every one.

Oh I wonder if Christ our Shepherd Divine
Doesn't work in the selfsame way,
By taking the dear little lambs to draw
The sheep that have gone astray?

Oftentimes He has tried, yes so very long,
To get us to follow His call
And when everything fails, He takes to Himself
The tiniest lamb of all.

To punish us? No! He loves us so much
That He died for our sins to atone,
But He hopes when the lambs are all safe in the fold,
That the sheep will follow Him home.

After she had read it a few times she handed it across the cot in which her 'tiny lamb' was battling for life, to Hertford, who was emotionally shattered as well.

He read it in silence, making no attempt to comment.

Phyllis reclaimed the poem and read it yet again. God was really speaking to her, convicting her.

So this was the message. God, in His infinite wisdom, had removed one of her lambs into His fold of joy and peace and freedom from pain, and He was in the process of carrying a second one home as well.

Could she, would she, follow?

Although she had been saved years before in Moira, she had lost her joy, her peace, her sense of direction. She was going round in spiritual circles. That was when she went anywhere at all.

Her Shepherd had called her once and she had followed Him gladly then. Now He was asking her to rise up and follow Him again. The Shepherd was taking her lambs, and in the process lovingly leading her home.

She found the first line of the last verse comforting. It dispelled a long held belief, a sneaking fear.

How easy it had been to convince herself that God

was punishing her for a lack of commitment, and for her backslidden life.

This was not so. God wasn't punishing her! He was tenderly calling her. There was a tremendous difference!

That evening Phyllis was frightened. It was horrible to feel so helpless, wanting to do something, but knowing there was nothing could be done.

Wendsley's condition was deteriorating rapidly, hour by hour. It seemed even minute by minute.

She knew in her heart he was going to die.

Nothing could prevent it now.

Chapter 24
MY WEE SOLDIER

Not only was Wendsley's condition so distressing for his distraught parents, but it also affected the whole wider family circle. They just couldn't believe it!

A steady soundless stream of relatives poured into the ward all that Wednesday night and early Thursday morning. They stood struck dumb, helpless with grief, watching the medical staff as they nursed little Wendsley, attending to his every need.

An ominous silence settled on the ward. It was like the muffling, smothering, all-pervasive fog outside.

Hertford and Phyllis were totally shattered. They were too upset to think about anything and absolutely powerless to do anything.

If only they could do something miraculous, or buy something marvellous or contact some mighty healer.

The reality was stark, they couldn't. Much as they would do anything they could, they were unable to alter the situation. They couldn't for one second stay the ebbing tide of their little one's life.

How true it was what the doctor had said. Wendsley was now in the hands of God. They had no choice but to leave him there.

The only things they could do now were the small and tender things. These included wiping his brow, combing his hair, holding his hand and straightening his bedclothes.

They performed these loving touches over and over again.

Four o'clock came and Phyllis was almost at breaking point. She left the ward to go back and seek solitude in the relatives' room. Her mother called in to comfort her a number of times.

Hertford joined her about forty minutes later. He was out of his mind as well and geared himself up for what he was about to say next by putting his arms round his weeping wife.

"I think you had better come in here now, Phyllis," he whispered, in a dry croaky voice. "The doctor says his pulse is getting very shallow. It won't be long now. Come with me, and we will go in together."

With that Hertford took Phyllis's shaking hand in his strong one, and they returned to the hush of the ward.

It was almost four-forty five, nine days to the minute from their eldest son had died, when the parent's approached their youngest son's bed, hand in hand.

Suddenly Wendsley gave a short sigh.

Then there was stillness. There was a monotonous hum from the heart monitor. The line was straight. The heartbeat had ceased.

Wendsley had passed away.

Simultaneously, Hertford and Phyllis both screeched, "Wendsley! Wendsley!"

Hertford lifted the body of his little son into a sitting position in the bed.

"My wee soldier! My wee man! Mummy and daddy love you! Oh, my wee man! My wee soldier!" He was unaware, in his anguish, that he was repeating the same phrases in quick succession.

A doctor came forward and removed the drips so the traumatised parents could spend some precious final moments with the frail earthly body in which their Wendsley had once dwelt.

The ward filled up with silent, sobbing relatives.

The only sounds were the sounds of grief. Some of this was open public weeping, and some of it was more muted. This was interspersed by a series of sighs and the rustle of paper handkerchiefs.

Wendsley and Thomas were together once more.

They were safe in the arms of Jesus, secure on the shoulders of the Shepherd.

It was marvellous for them. What a relief!

It was tragic for Hertford and Phyllis. What a catastrophe!

This utterly devastated mum and dad had lost two children in less than two weeks.

How could they ever cope with THIS?

Chapter 25
'YES, JESUS LOVES ME.'

The bewildered parents drove home without a word. The only sounds to be heard above the whirr of the engine were deep heavy sighs and an occasional vigorous blowing of the nose.

There was little left to say.

As they sped along Phyllis found that a verse of the poem which had been given to her the previous afternoon kept repeating itself in her mind. She couldn't seem to escape it.

'Oftentimes He has tried, yes, so very long

To get us to follow His call...' These words struck like a dagger into her heart. They were so true. Her whole thought pattern became dominated by these words, ringing in her brain.

Even the fuss they had left behind back at the hospital was out of her mind now. Something dramatic was happening. God was speaking directly to her.

Hertford was saved now. That was a blessing. She was glad about that, having prayed for him so earnestly when she was younger.

Now the tables were turned. Phyllis was suddenly the one in the throes of spiritual conviction.

There was no doubt she too had been saved, that night in Moira twelve years before. She had lost interest in the things of God, though, and carelessly and callously turned her back on Him.

The Good Shepherd was now graciously calling her again.

'And when everything fails, He takes to Himself
The tiniest lamb of all.'

Phyllis was heartbroken it had to come to this. God wanted her to return to Him so badly that He had taken to Himself her youngest child, her 'tiniest lamb of all.' This was not to punish her, as she had once imagined, but to lead her back to the fold.

They were both overwhelmed by grief when they drove up to the front of their bungalow. Everything was so still. There was an awesome, almost frightening, hush.

Nobody was around. Ford was being cared for by other relatives, and no one else had arrived. They were on their own.

Phyllis stood on the doorstep, weeping inconsolably.

Nine days before, when she had come home from hospital, grief stricken, and looked through the glass door and up the hall, Wendsley was lying there, rolling over and over.

She had been devastated then. Her big problem at that time was to know what to say to him about Thomas, his brother, playmate and friend. Now the hall was empty except for the cold, unsympathetic furniture standing around.

There was no sound.

No movement.

No life.

No Wendsley.

He had gone too.

Standing there shaking on the step, a voice seemed to say to her, "And what about you? Thomas is at home with me. Wendsley has joined him, at home in heaven. What about you? The lambs are both safe in My fold, Phyllis. Are you going to follow them?"

As the broken-hearted mother pushed the door open to enter the hall, her soul was drawn to God, She realised again this wasn't punishment. This was love. Caring love, patient love, Divine love.

Her Heavenly Father so much yearned for her return that He was drawing her gently to Him.

When she stepped into the empty hall of their echoingly empty bungalow, her legs left her. Phyllis was physically weak, emotionally distressed and spiritually shattered. Collapsing to her knees on the floor, she cried out in anguish, "I have had it, Lord. I can't go another step until I am sure I don't miss out on heaven."

Then came the tears of repentance, the deep remorse.

"Lord, I'm really sorry that Thomas and Wendsley had to give their lives to bring Hertford to You for salvation, and to bring me to my senses so that I would come back to You," she wailed.

Hertford had gone in past his wife by this time. He was in the kitchen, searching for something which he would never have dreamed of opening a month before. It was a hymn book.

"Lord, please give me back the joy of my salvation. I know You have never left me, but I have left You, let you down, made a mess of my life." Still the pathetic figure in the hall was praying passionately. "Lord, I cannot go on another minute without You. It is only You has brought me to this point, and only You can help me from here on in. I will need You every day, every hour, every single minute of my life until I see Thomas and Wendsley again. Please, please, help me, Lord."

As Phyllis struggled to her feet a sense of the presence of the Lord enfolded her. She was absolutely certain God had heard her plea.

He was answering already.

During her outpourings to God, she had noticed Hertford crossing from the kitchen into the living room. When she went to find him the scene that met her was both touching and reassuring.

Her husband was sitting on the rug in front of the fire.

The firelight made dancing patterns on his face. A hymn book lay open before him.

Flopping down beside Hertford, she put her arms around him. He stretched out an arm and pulled her towards him.

When she looked down at the open page of the hymn book Phyllis's eyes fixed on words she had once known off by heart, but hadn't sung, or heard sung, for years. They reminded her of childhood and rekindled childlike trust.

"Let's sing that, Hertford," she suggested, pointing to the hymn that had attracted her attention. "We will sing it for Thomas and Wendsley, for Ford and for us. How true it is."

With tears of deep sorrow, mingled with tears of genuine relief, they sat close together in the firelight and sang huskily.

"Jesus loves me, this I know,
For the Bible tells me so,
Little ones to Him belong,
They are weak but He is strong."

This proved a tremendous boost to Phyllis and acted as a tonic to both of them. It gave them a definite sense of purpose, combined with a strange sense of peace.

They were united in grief.

They were united by human affection.

Now they were united in their desire to live for Christ and rejoice in His wonderful love.

No matter what could happen in the days ahead they were prepared to face the uncertainty of the future in the absolute certainty of the truth of the chorus,

"Yes, Jesus loves me,
Yes, Jesus loves me,
Yes, Jesus loves me,
The Bible tells me so."

Chapter 26
SOME PARTY IN HEAVEN

Their sacred singing session was soon to be interrupted.

Mourners started to arrive at the house. Hertford and Phyllis just couldn't seem to believe it. It was so unreal.

Here they were, nine days on from the shock of the death of Thomas seeing the same kind-hearted people coming to say the same tender-hearted things to sympathise with them at the death of Wendsley.

At nine o'clock the undertaker arrived with the tiny white coffin. "In all my years in this job," he told the grieving parents, "I have never had an experience like this before."

He was so genuinely upset that he just asked for Wendsley's full name and age. He thought he could cope with nearly every challenge his work presented but this was proving extremely difficult. Nine days before he had looked down to see a little boy tugging at his trouser leg. Now he was compiling his death notice for the paper.

He was almost overcome.

"He was Wendsley John Arnold and he was just three years and two months old," Hertford told him. "He was born on the 29th September 1986."

With that information quickly noted, the undertaker left, only to return two days later for the funeral.

Saturday, 25th November began with the same choking fog that had merged day into night for weeks on end.

By mid-morning, however, the fog had lifted and the sun came out. The mourners walked from the bungalow to the church in Donacloney in the first sunshine they had seen for days.

The lane was lined with men waiting to join the funeral. Many of them stood in the same positions as they had done nine days before. It was uncanny.

The whole day seemed to be an action replay of the day Thomas was buried just over a week before..

There was one important difference, though, and it had taken place in lives of the two chief mourners. Since that day Hertford had been saved and Phyllis had been restored to the Lord.

What a change it made!

Now, as they followed Wendsley's little coffin to the church they realised what it was all about.

Thomas had gone and he hadn't come back. That was in spite of his parents' vain hope that one day he would just reappear somehow.

They knew now that Wendsley had gone too. This was for real. He wouldn't sit in his high chair or roll on the floor again, either.

Their profound sorrow and many tears of that second funeral in less than a fortnight were accompanied by a deep sense of inner peace. They knew that where Thomas was Wendsley was, and that was where they were both going as well. What a consolation.

As they sat together in the back of the funeral car on the way home from the cemetery in Dromore, dusk was falling. The sky was swallowing up the red ball of sun. Everywhere appeared momentarily aflame.

The heavens were declaring the glory of God.

It seemed as though their Heavenly Father was putting his seal to the end of a chapter in their lives.

The parents held hands. They were acutely aware of the

presence of God, the Mighty Creator and their Saviour.

Phyllis looked across at Hertford, tears glinting golden on her cheeks in the afterglow from the sunset sky. "There must be some party in heaven right now," she remarked.

Chapter 27

BLACK CHRISTMAS

The darkest days of winter followed immediately after the funerals.

Ford, who had been at home from school for a week, went back.

Hertford had arranged for his father and brothers to look after the chicken house for him for a few days. Then he went back to his work down the yard.

With her husband and son out of the house Phyllis decided to do some cleaning. It would keep her mind occupied. As she worked her way along the hall with the vacuum cleaner she stopped at the door of the boys' bedroom and looked in.

The toys and teddy bears were still there. They stood, sat and lay respectfully around, as though awaiting the return of their owners.

The room was spic and span. The room was clean and tidy. The room was empty.

Phyllis switched off the cleaner. She felt so guilty.

Thomas had gone, never to come back. Wendsley had gone, never to come back.

Yet everything in the household appeared to have returned to normal. Ford had gone back to school. Hertford was down in the chicken house again, and she was cleaning the house as she had always done.

Phyllis stood in the hall and prayed. "Lord, if You are really here, please reveal Yourself to me."

Too unsettled to continue with the vacuuming she went into the kitchen and sat down at the end of the table. She felt ashamed of herself, lonely and all mixed up.

Reaching up to a nearby shelf she lifted down her Bible. She had never been in the habit of looking for verses at random, but on this particular occasion she felt it was the thing to do. Flicking slowly through the precious book in front of her she prayed, "Lord give me a verse."

As the pages rustled over, her eyes rested on words which seemed to bounce off the page to meet her. The Lord had answered her request. He had given her 'a verse.'

It was Ecclesiastes chapter 11, verse 5.

Phyllis read the words over and over again. She hadn't known until that moment they were in the Bible.

'As thou knowest not what is the way of the spirit, nor how the bones do grow in the womb of her that is with child: e'en so thou knowest not the works of God who maketh all.'

That was her verse, her direct revelation from God.

Over the previous six years Phyllis had often been tempted to question the ways and works of God. This verse told her she could never attempt to know or understand His design for her life.

She could, though, accept it as best, and this was a tremendous consolation.

The works of God who had made everything were away beyond her comprehension, yet He knew about her, and cared for her as well. Someday she would find out the reason for it all, but not right now, not in the meantime and probably not even on earth.

Some of the most trying times for Hertford and Phyllis in those early December days were when Ford, aged four-and-a half, told them how much he missed his brothers. One evening, after they had eaten their meal but before they left the table, he said, completely out of the blue, "I miss Thomas and Wendsley, but I know they are away to heaven."

After a short pause, which created a silence that could almost be touched, he went on to ask about something which he had obviously been contemplating for some time. "Will they be fixed when they come back?" he enquired.

In his childish mind he had imagined heaven to be some kind of celestial service centre where less than perfect humans were repaired and then returned to their families

It proved difficult for his loving, grieving parents to explain to him tenderly that Thomas and Wendsley were already 'fixed.' They were with Jesus in heaven and had been changed. But no. They wouldn't be coming back.

Hertford and Phyllis proceeded to explain to him how they expected to see their other two boys again in heaven, but this could only happen after they themselves had also died.

There were up days and down days for all three of them as time went on. For many people the bleak mid-winter is brightened by the onset of Christmas. Hertford and Phyllis used to love the buzz of the season, planning presents and surprises for the boys, decorating the house and purchasing and preparing festive food.

That year they dreaded those once exciting weeks approaching.

During the third week of December both parents decided that Ford would have as enjoyable a Christmas as possible, despite all that had happened. They would buy him a good present. He had told them both what he wanted. It was a racing car set.

Although they found themselves unable to summon up any enthusiasm for Christmas shopping, Hertford and Phyllis drove into Portadown and stopped outside a department store. The still-heartbroken mother went in and up the stairs. She knew exactly what she wanted.

Jingly Christmas music was playing, and the store was crowded with happy but somewhat harassed parents being lobbied by happy but nonetheless insistent children.

Observing what must have been a look of bewilderment on the prospective customer's face, an assistant stepped across to her and asked if he could be of any help.

Phyllis enquired if they sold racing car sets.

"Oh yes, we have a whole selection of them," the assistant replied. He was both friendly and eager to please. "Have you any idea what model it is you want?"

Phyllis couldn't stay there a moment longer. Seeing all those children with their parents was just too much for her. Muttering something about having "to see" she made for the stairs.

Hertford was waiting in the car outside. "Have they not got them?" he asked, when his wife collapsed into the passenger seat beside him, empty-handed.

"They have them OK in the place upstairs," Phyllis replied. "But I couldn't stick it in there. I had to come out. You may go in and buy it."

Hertford did just that. He went into the shop and up the stairs two steps at a time. After a hasty look around he bought what he considered the most suitable racing track for his surviving son, in double quick time.

Returning to the car in less than ten minutes, much to his wife's surprise for she knew how busy the shop was, Hertford opened the boot and tossed in a black bin bag.

That was Christmas 1989 all wrapped up for Ford.

Significantly, it was wrapped up in black.

The grief-stricken parents couldn't possibly ignore the memory of Thomas and Wendsley at Christmas either. Happy recollections of their faces, which seemed to glow unusually brightly when presents appeared, haunted sleepless nights. They wanted to buy something for them also.

To fulfil this anguished desire they drove to Lisburn on Christmas Eve and purchased two plain holly wreaths, draped with red ribbons.

On their way home they placed them on the simple double grave in Dromore.

That was Christmas 1989 all wrapped up for Thomas and Wendsley.

Sadly, it was wrapped up with wreaths.

Chapter 28
DEAD LEAVES - NEW LIFE

The new year, 1990, began just as gloomily as the old one had ended.

Times were hard. Days were short, and cold. Nights were long. Things were tough.

5th January would have been Thomas's sixth birthday.

That afternoon, his heavy-hearted parents removed the holly wreaths and placed six red roses on the grave in Dromore.

How could they ever forget? When would they ever accept?

In mid-January Phyllis took a walk out around the bungalow one morning. She was upset and unsettled and felt she must be on the move. Ford had just gone off to school. Hertford had been down at the chicken house for some time. It was still only nine-thirty.

The previous night had been bitterly cold and the ground was covered with hoar frost which lay like an off-white sheet in the morning light. Phyllis didn't notice the extreme cold. She was preoccupied, totally absorbed in thought.

As she rounded the corner of the bungalow she looked across at the flower bed. Her eye was drawn to what had once been a clump of carnations. What had been a succession of glorious colour the previous summer had become a mound of drab and drooping vegetation.

The grey-white spikes of the carnation leaves hung limp and lifeless, covered by frosty rime. Even the stalks seemed to have flopped out, given up. They lay black and brittle on the rock-hard soil.

Whether it was the pattern of the frost on the carnation leaves, or the effect of the frost on the carnation plant, something compelled Phyllis to walk over, bend down and take a closer look.

She noticed a solitary stalk, lying at an angle to the main clump and looking singularly sorry for itself. Reaching forward, she tried to lift it up, but it broke off in her hand.

All of a sudden Thomas and Wendsley came before her in a vivid recollection. She could picture clearly in her mind the little faces she used to put cream on. She could feel the delicate strands of the wispy hair she used to comb, time and time again.

Standing there in the winter garden, clutching a broken, lifeless, carnation stalk, Phyllis was transfixed.

Lapsing into reverie, she felt she could almost smell her sons' fresh skin after they had been bathed. Their hearty laughter rang in her ears. What she would have given at that moment to have seen them again in the flesh... to have touched them... to have looked into their happy faces... to...

Glancing down at the flower bed again returned her abruptly to reality. Different thoughts, infinitely less pleasant ones, swamped the troubled mother's mind.

"They are dead. In the soil. Brittle and decaying, just like those plants. Once in bloom, now dead and gone. They will turn to dust. Don't kid yourself. You will never see them again."

Having blitzed her fragile emotions with such disturbing thoughts, her mind then proceeded to recreate some graphic images.

She recalled two dreadful days in November.

She went back to Dromore, back to a cemetery.

She heard the hollow thump of the soil on one little coffin. Then on another.

Warm tears overflowed on to cold cheeks. Then the questioning began for yet another time.

"Why did all this have to happen to us? Why did we have to lose both of them?"

Phyllis was overwhelmed with a mixture of anger and depression.

"Now we are in our bungalow. Now, at last, we can cope financially. When we were just coming to the position where we could really enjoy our two dear little boys they have been taken away from us."

Thus ran her thoughts.

Eventually realising that she was becoming stiff with cold she dropped her limp carnation and retraced her steps round to the back door. Walking up the gentle ramp especially designed for the boys' wheelchairs, she cried out in agony.

"Lord, please, please, don't let me think like this," she pleaded. "I don't want to think like this. Help me, Lord, to trust in you."

Despite her impassioned prayer, and despite her deliberate efforts to resign herself to what she knew to be the will of the Lord, Phyllis continued to be bombarded by unsettling thoughts for days and months to come.

So too did Hertford. He tried to cope in a more silent, manly fashion, but it was hard. Very, very hard.

On a number of occasions during that lonely winter he appeared up into the house, having abandoned his work on the farm. A profound emptiness had created an extreme restlessness in his spirit.

"Come on," he said to Phyllis on many such occasions, "We will go over to Dromore."

Having stopped somewhere to buy flowers on the way,

they placed two little bunches tenderly on the grave with the two little coffins in it. They then sat there, wrapped up against the winter weather, silently weeping for half an hour. Sometimes it was longer than that, up to and occasionally more than, an hour.

Visitors decreased in numbers as the days progressed. Hertford and Phyllis kept up bravely while they were in, chatting to them. After all it was more than two months now since the boys had passed away. They didn't want people to consider them weak, or even worse, sickly sentimental.

Put your trust in God. Look ahead, not back. Face up to it fair and square. Wasn't that what they were supposed to do?

It was what they appeared to do while the well-wishers sat and talked. The visitors hadn't reached the end of the lane on their way home, however, until Hertford and Phyllis exploded into floods of tears.

They even went shopping away from their local stores. The weekend groceries were bought in the more distant towns of Lisburn or Banbridge. It didn't matter to them where they went as long as the other people with the trolleys and the check-out operators were all strangers.

It was hard to retain composure, they found, when selecting breakfast cereals, if some very thoughtful and genuinely sympathetic person would approach them and say, "Hertford and Phyllis," or it could be, "Mr. and Mrs. Arnold. I was awfully sorry to hear about your two wee boys..."

Apart from their trips to the graveyard in Dromore and short shopping ventures to local venues, most of their time was spent in and around the house. Socialising of any sort had become a problem, well-nigh an impossibility.

Hertford and Phyllis were finding the loss, the loneliness, the awful emptiness, the utter sense of futility, desperately painful.

It was in April when Phyllis decided to take a walk around the bungalow again one morning. It was spring. The daffodils had reappeared and their yellow trumpets surrounded by green spears were brightening up the lane.

It was almost lunch time, but still cool. As the despairing mother wandered slowly along, her eyes rested on the bunch of carnations whose frosted lifelessness had arrested her during the winter.

What a transformation! Life had returned! The grey spiky leaves were stiff and straight. On looking more closely she noticed that a few buds were beginning to swell at the ends of the lengthening stalks.

Phyllis felt elated. Desperation disappeared for an instant.

Closing her hands and raising her arms to God she exclaimed, "Praise the Lord! That's it!"

The sudden recollection of the realisation that Thomas and Wendsley would not just decay in the cold earth forever put a different complexion on things. God, who could restore frosted, blackened carnation stalks to life would restore Thomas and Wendsley's bodies and change them too. It would not present Him with a serious problem to "fix them" for Ford.

Then when resurrected bodies were reunited with happy souls she and Hertford would rejoin them. They would be forever with the Lord, and each other, in perfection and bliss.

With all that to look forward to, why should she feel so depressed?

Thomas and Wendsley had never appeared depressed. They had never once looked unhappy. They had just laughed and played and smiled for most of their short lives.

Their parents could never have been any help to them while they were alive if they had been down in the dumps all the time. They certainly weren't going to be any good to each other or anyone else either, now, if they were determined to spend the remainder of their days simply moping around.

There was the promise, and the prospect, of new life. They must be positive about the future, whatever it held.

When Hertford came into the kitchen, almost an hour later, for his lunch, Phyllis was bursting to tell him about her discovery.

"You remember back in January, Hertford," she began, "I told you about an experience I had out in the garden, when I saw the dead plants with the frost all over them. How I was shocked and sickened when I thought that Thomas and Wendsley were just like those plants. I imagined them dead and gone, disintegrating into dust in the soil."

"Yes, I remember that," her husband replied. He remembered it well in fact, for neither of them had slept a wink for two nights after it.

"Well, I was out there again just before you came up," she continued, "and you will never believe it! The plant that was then just a big dead clump has now all perked up. In fact there are wee buds coming out on it again!

"Yes, but is that not the way plants go? They die off in the winter and perk up again in the spring," Hertford replied. Obviously he hadn't grasped the deeper meaning of the illustration.

"That's true. It is," Phyllis agreed. "But can you not see what I am getting at? I believe that God used it to teach us, well me anyway, a lesson, and here's what it is...

God can bring new life. He can make dead things live. Thomas and Wendsley aren't dead. Their souls are alive and one day He will give new life to their bodies and they will be recreated in heaven. Our two little boys will be perfect!"

Phyllis paused to gauge her husband's reaction to this revelation. He sat gazing at her thoughtfully, idly tapping a spoon on the table. She hadn't told him anything he didn't already know, and which she should have already known also.

It was the freshness with which it came that he warmed to, however. Phyllis had spoken with more fire than he had seen her display for anything for six months. This seemed to indicate a return of the enthusiastic wife he had once known.

She wasn't finished yet either. There was more to come. "I also believe God has shown me we ought to be more positive about things," she went on. "We shouldn't be depressed and moody all the time. God doesn't expect it. The boys would never have wanted it. So why don't we face the future? We must do our best for God, for each other, for Ford and for everybody else we can, trusting Him to help us."

Hertford continued pensive. He still hadn't spoken on the matter.

It was right, he knew. It was sensible, but it would be tough.

"OK," he declared, a trifle hesitantly. "We will do our best, as you say."

They smiled bravely at each other.

God had spoken to them again, this time through His creation.

Chapter 29
COTTAGE CATERING

Not long after her two garden encounters with the ways
and works of God, the creator and sustainer of new life, Phyllis
remarked to her husband one day, "You know, Hertford, I am
bored in the house. I can have all my housework done before
you come up for your lunch and then I have far too much
time on my hands. That gives me time to think. I want to be
positive about our situation, but I really need something to
keep me busy all the time. It would help if I could be occupied
every hour of the day."

Phyllis had come to realise that unless she could focus on
a wider range of activity, memories of Thomas and Wendsley
were set to dominate the thoughts of all her waking moments.
She was trying ever so hard to be forward-looking, but so far
it wasn't working.

"Why don't we start making the trifles again?" Hertford
suggested, almost immediately. He was all for doing his best
to be more constructive in his outlook, but he could see his
wife was finding it tough.

There were a number of times in the previous few months
when he had considered getting back to the trifle-making,
even if only in a small way. It would give them both, but
particularly Phyllis, something definite to do. Rewarding,
positive thinking for her at that particular time was bound to
prove an uphill journey, all the way. She needed help.

Hertford had the broken heart of a father but with the
chicken house to occupy his mind and energy. Phyllis had

the broken heart of a mother but with nothing to do other than housework, which she did mechanically. To her it was required, rather than rewarding, work.

So now that she had expressed her problem so concisely, he seized the opportunity to express what he considered the ideal solution.

"I was wondering about that too, Hertford," came the response, after a moment or two of reflection. "But maybe it's a bit soon yet. We will think about it for a wee while."

The "wee while" they decided to leave to allow them to "think about it" turned out to be exactly that. It was a very short time, no more than a couple of days.

One evening the phone rang. It was a distributor to whom they had been selling trifles the previous summer. His request was simple.

"Could you start supplying me again with the trifles we were selling last year?" he enquired. "I am constantly being asked for them."

It was arranged that he should call at their home the following Thursday evening to discuss the matter further. Could this be a Heavenly confirmation of a Hertford suggestion?

When the distributor called that evening and told them of the constant enquiries he had been receiving about the trifles, Hertford and Phyllis agreed to start making them again.

Here was something they could do. This was something they KNEW they could do. It was something to keep both hands and minds occupied.

They agreed that the first order would be delivered early the next week. This commitment led to instant activity. It meant back to the planning, back to the buying and back to the Aga.

The Aga was the hard bit, and the first night was the worst.

The smell of melting jelly in the kitchen seemed to emphasise an emptiness in the house. There was nobody waiting for the leftover jelly. There would be nobody to get excited about a few spoonfuls of extra cream.

As they stood stirring, then pouring jelly, on the first evening back, tears flowed freely.

Happy memories flooded into busy minds.

Herford summarised how he felt to Phyllis at one stage. "I know this is good for us. It is probably the best thing for us. My problem is that I just feel somehow as if I am walking over the boys' grave," was how he put it.

They were both experiencing a similar sensation.

It was as though the body was galloping ahead, proclaiming, "This is great! I'm glad to be doing something for a change. Keep it up!"

All the time, however, the mind was holding each one of them back with the reins which had 'Guilt' stamped all over them. These reins of guilt transmitted messages like "Think about the boys. How can you be so thoughtless, and appear so normal? You are letting them down, neglecting their memory."

As they retired to bed after all the jelly and custard and cream involvement of that first evening back trifle making, Herford and Phyllis felt sad, yet strangely satisfied. Their hearts were still sore, but their minds and hands had been restored to a former degree of usefulness.

How would the trifles take off this time?

It would be well, if their friend had gauged the situation correctly. If what he had been telling them was true there was an obvious niche in the market eagerly awaiting the reintroduction of their kitchen-produced delicacies.

They would see. Time would tell.

Again they didn't have long to wait.

The distributor had been right. There was a demand. Orders began to roll in, and increase, daily.

Soon a previous and familiar work pattern was re-established. Phyllis saw Ford off to school and started to set up the trifles for the orders to be delivered that day. Hertford then came up from the chicken house, had a shower, donned the whites, and did his bit, the packaging and delivery.

In a week's time they were on the phone with Heather, asking her to come over and help them once more. She readily agreed, and that made three of them.

All hands were needed as the orders continued to pour in. The word had spread like wildfire. "Those wee trifles are back in the shops."

As they became busier day by day, Hertford and Phyllis came to realise that God had devised His own programme of occupational therapy for them. They had become proficient in making and marketing trifles five months before the boys died. God knew He would be calling their little ones home to Himself and had, in His wisdom, arranged something for them to do.

The grieving parents began gradually to appreciate that they weren't "walking over the boys' graves" as they had first imagined. On the contrary, they were in fact implementing God's plan for their lives.

As time went on and the summer progressed the busy couple were getting very little sleep. Long hours at work and short nights in bed became the order of each day.

They employed more staff. Soon there were eight of them coming and going throughout the day. Hundreds of trifles were being turned out daily in the bungalow kitchen and 'the work place' became very cramped.

Throughout the increased activity of those summer days there were times when Hertford and Phyllis would suddenly remember the boys. Something would grab their attention unexpectedly. It could be something simple that stopped them dead in their tracks.

It may have been the smell of melting jelly. It could have been a spoon, lying tilted at a crazy angle in a stainless steel bowl containing the remnants of some unscraped-out cream. It could have been the empty doorway where Wendsley used to sit, propped up, watching, waiting and anticipating.

A seemingly inconsequential word, or action, or smell, or situation, could bring the tide of nostalgia flooding back. They used to stop, as individuals, at such moments and thank God for the boys, and for their memory, before proceeding with the job in hand.

What a job it had become, too. The demand just seemed to keep on growing. During the summer it became evident that in order to supply all the shops and supermarkets expressing an interest in stocking their product they would have to expand their operation. A purpose-built factory unit was the only solution.

This meant sitting down with architects and advisors and drawing up plans for a 1,000 square foot facility.

Hertford and Phyllis consoled themselves with the thought that when the new unit was complete life would become a little easier for them.

That's not what happened, though.

Their new trifle-producing mini-factory was fully operational in four months, but in that period the market had increased apace. Life now, even with increased staff and automated machinery, became more and more frenetic.

In a short time the new unit proved to be too small to cope with the volume of business they were doing. Demand for new lines meant that not only were the original lines being produced in ever increasing quantities, but they added cheesecakes and puddings to their product range as well.

The unit was doubled in size.

The staff was doubled in size.

Very soon there were 20 full-time members of the production team. Outlets all over Ireland were being supplied. Plans were drawn up for a much larger modern factory in Dromore, Co. Down.

Hertford and Phyllis were amazed at the rapid expansion of their business interests. God had been so good to them.

One of their main concerns in the earlier days was attending business meetings with high powered executives from supermarket chains in shiny offices somewhere. They reckoned themselves to be just ordinary country people who lived down at the end of a big long lane in the absolute heart of nowhere.

What would they say? They were by no means posh, and they couldn't put it on. Would the bossman understand them even?!

They needn't have worried. Time and time again they proved the wonderful grace of God.

The country couple were given words which they had never used before, to say, and they were given an understanding of business principles they never before knew existed.

Unexpected doors opened without the slightest push.

When they placed their future in God's hands, they realised that the One who had taken their two little lambs to Himself, was still their loving Shepherd.

It was also exciting, but humbling, to prove practically the truth of the Saviour's own words from the Sermon on the Mount...

"But seek ye first the kingdom of God and his righteousness: and all these things shall be added unto you." Matthew 6: 33.

Chapter 30
'THIS IS MY STORY'

'This is my story, this is my song,
Praising my Saviour all the day long.'
(Frances van Alstyne.)

One day early in 1991 a Christian neighbour came into the factory where Hertford and Phyllis were working away. He had a proposal to put to them.

"I was wondering if either of you, or if both of you, would consider telling your story, 'giving your testimony' if you like to call it that, in the wee Mission Hall up the road?" he asked.

The young couple looked at each other in silence. Here was something else they could do. It would be something more for God than themselves. They could 'praise their Saviour' if they accepted this invitation.

When he had received an assuring nod from his wife, Hertford replied, "OK. We will give it a go. Mind you we have never done it before, but I suppose everybody has to start somewhere."

Their first meeting in that local Mission Hall with a very small congregation proved to be a nervous, stumbling start.

There was warmth in the meeting, though. There was feeling. There was God. The encouraging comments from their friends and neighbours on the way out helped them appreciate how worthwhile it had been.

Hertford and Phyllis went home happy that evening. They felt on fire for the Lord. They had been able to stand up and witness to His saving, guiding and keeping power, in their own townland. It was wonderful.

News travels fast in country parts. It wasn't long until they had received their second invitation. Their first meeting had been on Hertford's home ground in Donacloney. Their second one was to be held in a hall in Dollingstown, the village where Phyllis had been brought up.

This second meeting differed from the first only in the fact that the crowd was much bigger. The hall was packed to capacity. In the end, a few latecomers ended up standing around the walls.

From the very moment they began to speak Hertford and Phyllis felt an amazing sense of the presence of God. As they related the step-by-step dealings of God through the traumas and triumphs of their lives, people were moved to tears.

Soon there wasn't a dry eye in the hall.

God was at work.

Again, after the meeting, people told them how the story had touched their hearts. And again they felt that glow of satisfaction. It was a renewed sense of gratitude at having been able to return praise to God for His gracious guidance in their lives.

Very soon the lives of Hertford and Phyllis had taken on a second pattern.

This time, however, it wasn't a work pattern. It wasn't an early-rising, jelly-melting, cream-spreading, tub-filling, van-driving pattern.

It was a witness pattern. It was a meeting-going, heart-searching, Christ-exalting, tear-producing pattern.

Hertford and Phyllis were soon being asked to tell 'their story' in many places all over Northern Ireland. Usually someone would ring up and speak to either of them. The caller would most likely, but not always, be from a church group.

"We have heard about you from Mrs. Blank in Ballymacsomething and we were wondering if you would be free to come and speak to our group? We feel your story could be a great help to some of the friends in our fellowship. They have been going through a rough time this last while. We meet on a Tuesday night. You could have your pick of a couple of dates – either the 14th of March or the 11th of April..." was the essence of a typical request.

Hertford and Phyllis never refused an invitation if at all possible. They were afraid to. If God, who meant so much to them, had led somebody to ask them to the Backwoods Bible Church, they would go. Perhaps there would be someone there whom He had planned to encourage through them.

They spoke to very large audiences, and to rather small ones. They spoke in city churches and country halls.

It was nearly always their experience that there was at least one grieving soul in the congregation to whom their testimony proved an inspiration, or a hesitant heart to whom it came as a challenge.

Different, heartbroken people stood, silently weeping, holding tightly on to the hand of either of the speakers. "That was great," they would say, sobbing, "That was a marvellous help to me. You see I lost a son, or a daughter, when he was three, or six, or nine. I am still struggling to come to terms with it."

Others wrote letters, phoned, or even stopped Hertford or Phyllis on the street. Every time anything like this happened they gave all the praise to God.

This was, and is, their story – praising their Saviour, all the day, every day, long.

Though many people have declared themselves inspired by the testimony, the greatest help, and challenge of any evening is to the speakers themselves, Hertford and Phyllis.

It makes them feel so close to God, and to each other, and to Thomas and Wendsley.

Every testimony meeting still brings the two boys back to life for a brief, but precious, period, in their hearts. They often drive to a meeting in tears, considering and discussing who is going to say what.

Occasionally their route to a meeting takes them past the cemetery in Dromore.

They slow down and look over. "Boys, we are on our way to talk about you both tonight," one of them says. They then accelerate, wipe away a tear, and continue to that evening's engagement.

That family bond, though severed for a while, is very evident when Hertford and Phyllis speak. This is what has drawn so many suffering souls to identify with them.

Hertford often quotes verse 21 from Philippians chapter 1. *"For to me, to live is Christ, and to die is gain."*

"To me, to live is Christ, is why we are here tonight," he proceeds to explain. "We want to tell you more about Him. And to die is gain. That is what we are looking forward to. It is the gain that can only come to us after death. That will be to meet the Lord, then Thomas and Wendsley again. They are now with the Lord and we are going to join them there. Isn't it marvellous to think that the first words that either of them ever spoke were to the Saviour? And the first steps they ever took were when they went to walk with Him."

Phyllis has never forgotten those who encouraged her through the most difficult days and the most trying experiences. She will always be grateful to them for the gracious way in which they pointed her back to God.

Thus when she speaks she often embraces the opportunity to succour those who are passing through testing times. She empathises naturally with those who are coping daily with the increased demands of a child or children with special educational needs.

"If there is anyone here who is the father or mother, sister or brother, granny or granda, uncle or aunt, to a child with special needs, count that a privilege," she tells audiences tenderly. "He or she is extremely special, for he or she is a gift from God."

Herford and Phyllis both continue to live the message. They convey with such feeling the wealth of love their two 'gifts from God' brought to them in their short lives. They often refer to Thomas and Wendsley as their 'two little angels,' because after the boys' death someone gave them a book by Helen Steiner Rice.

Their favourite poem from that collection, and one which seemed to describe their life and experience so accurately was this:

BLESSINGS IN DISGUISE ARE DIFFICULT TO RECOGNISE.

God sends His 'little angels'
in many forms and guises.
They come as lovely miracles
that God alone devises.
For He does nothing without purpose,
everything's a perfect plan
To fulfil in bounteous measure
all He ever promised man –
And every 'little angel'
with a body bent and broken
Or a little mind retarded
or little words unspoken,
Is just God's way of trying

to reach and touch the hand
Of all who do not know Him
and cannot understand
That often through an angel
whose wings will never fly
The Lord is pointing out the way
to His eternal sky
Where there will be no handicaps
of body, soul or mind,
And where all limitations
will be dropped and left behind –
So accept these 'little angels'
as gifts from God above,
And thank Him for this lesson
in FAITH and HOPE and LOVE.

Chapter 31
THE BEST NEWS!

"I have no mummy or daddy but I am not worried about that. The Lord looks after me." Such was the testimony of an eleven-year-old African boy.

In May 1994 Hertford and Phyllis took Ford along to hear the African Children's Choir in Ballynahinch, Co. Down. One by one some of those young children told of their faith in God. Their faith vibrated and radiated as they spoke and sang.

It touched Ford's heart.

On the way home in the car he was very quiet. When they stopped at the front of the bungalow, Phyllis jumped out of the car. She ran round to the back of it in time to speak to her husband before Ford got out.

"Say nothing, but Ford is crying in there!" she whispered.

Just before bedtime Ford sat, legs tucked under him, on the rocking-chair in front of the Aga. There was an occasional squeak from the chair as he rocked to and fro, obviously deep in thought. "Could we not bring some of those wee children here?" he asked at length. "They have no mummies or daddies and we have plenty of room."

Hertford and Phyllis didn't reply at once.

They couldn't. They were struck dumb, rendered speechless.

Ford, who was by then their one and only son, was clearly upset. His parents were soon to discover there was something more, something further, something deeper, on his mind.

"Mummy, I would love a wee brother," he blurted out

finally, with a sob and a sigh.

His mummy knew how he felt. She couldn't hold back a tear.

He must be desperately lonely. What could she say, though? How could she explain?

"Only God knows if He is going to give us any more children," she told him gently. "He alone knows whether you will have another brother or not."

Later, after Ford had gone to bed, his mum and dad sat up talking, far into the night. "Isn't it an awful pity of Ford on his own?" Phyllis asked repeatedly. She didn't need Hertford, or anybody else for that matter, to provide her with the answer to her question.

Yes. Of course it was 'an awful pity of Ford on his own' but what were the implications of anything else? What would they do if they had another child and he or she turned out to be handicapped? And then died?

It had happened with two-thirds of their family so far. Could they cope with all that again?

That night before she went to bed, Phyllis prayed.

That night as she tossed and turned sleeplessly in bed, Phyllis prayed.

For many days and nights to come, Phyllis prayed.

"Lord, if You want us to have another baby, please reveal it to us. Only you can give us another child, and we want Your will for our lives," was her simple request.

The summer passed quickly. It was very busy. Cottage Catering had become a household name and for five days every week Hertford and Phyllis rose early and retired late, just to keep abreast of demand.

Days became shorter. The warm days of summer made way for the crisp days of autumn. Winter was on its way.

It was November, 1994.

Late one evening as the ever-active couple tidied up around the kitchen, Phyllis shared a growing suspicion with her husband. "I think I should tell you Hertford," she announced rather bluntly, "I am nearly sure I am pregnant again."

Hertford stopped what he was doing abruptly. He turned, rested against the bench, and folded his arms. No words came for a moment.

Then he retorted, apparently incredulously, and unusually gruffly too, "Catch yourself on, ma, you couldn't be!"

"Maybe you think I couldn't be, Hertford," his wife replied. She knew him only too well, and had anticipated this kind of kneejerk reaction.

"Maybe you think I couldn't be," she went on, echoing her opening statement for emphasis. "But I am almost certain that I am!"

Hertford was stunned. He started to walk about, taking short steps from here to there, and back. An agitated mind in motion set agitated feet in motion. The reluctant prospective father-to-be ended up like a fairground roundabout. He went endlessly up and down and round and round without ever getting anywhere.

He picked up things that didn't need to be picked up and set them down again where they didn't need to go.

"What are we going to do?" he kept asking. It was now his turn to repeat what he had said, not though for emphasis, but through nervous excitement.

"What are we doing to do?" "What ARE we going to do?"

The "what if?" doubts had begun to sneak in already, before the pregnancy had even been confirmed. The becoming increasingly hassled husband then decided that if Phyllis wasn't one hundred per cent convinced she was right, it was certainly time they both knew for sure.

"Is there any way you can be really certain? Can you find out for definite, I mean?" he enquired.

Hertford was a man of the soil, of the chicken house, and latterly of a factory full of trifles, but he wasn't well up in matters gynaecological.

"Yes, I suppose there is," Phyllis volunteered. "I could have a scan."

"Well arrange for a scan as soon as you can," her husband instructed, his poetic turn of phrase occurring more by chance than choice. "Then we will know."

Phyllis did as he requested and when the results of the scan were revealed they were positive. It was true, having now been medically confirmed. She was expecting another baby.

Hertford had by that time recovered from the initial shock and his attitude to the situation had become more controlled. He was glad for them, and for Ford. This must be, it just had to be, the will of God, he reckoned.

Hertford and Phyllis hugged each other after they heard the result. It was great. Another baby would provide a much longed-for brother or sister for Ford.

But what if?

They would have to tell Ford when a suitable opportunity presented itself. He would have to be the first to know, when the time was right.

It was late one night, shortly before Christmas, that Hertford and Phyllis were sitting in bed, chatting. They knew that Ford, in his bedroom across the hall, wasn't asleep. It seemed to be the ideal time to let him into the secret.

"Ford, are you still awake?" his mum called.

"Yes. Why?" came the almost guilty-sounding response.

"Come in here a minute then, we have something to tell you," Phyllis continued.

In two seconds their son was standing at the end of their

bed. His hair was sticking out all over the place and his eyes were bright. Obviously sleep had still been very far away.

"What is it?" he enquired breathlessly. All he could think of was his Christmas present list.

"Sit down on the end of the bed there, son," Hertford suggested. "Your mummy has good news for you."

"Good news. What is it, mummy? Please tell me!" Ford begged. There could be no mistaking the sense of eager anticipation in his voice.

"What? Guess what. Go on, have a guess. What do you think it could be?" Phyllis thought she would play the 'Guess what?' game with him. This had been a standard, just for fun practice when opening presents, both at Christmas and his birthday, for the previous few years.

"Ach mummy, stop keeping me going. I haven't a clue. What is it?" Ford was excited now, but becoming impatient. "Do you remember the night we went to hear the African Children's Choir, away back in May?" Phyllis became serious as she began to explain. "Can you remember what you told us that night?"

"Yes, I do," Ford replied after only a moment's hesitation. "I said I would like a wee brother."

"That's right," his mum went on. His dad and she were both amused at the quizzical look which had come over his face. "And I told you that only God knew if we were going to have another baby or not. Well, we ARE going to have another baby next year. You are going to have a little brother or sister!"

Ford sat motionless for a few seconds until the full impact of the message sank in. Then he jumped off the end of the bed and hugged his mummy, much to her surprise, for he had never, up until that minute, been an emotionally demonstrative sort of child.

He was crying again, but it was for joy this time.

On releasing Phyllis from the bear hug, he took to running up and down the hall. He darted into his own bedroom, then his parents' room, and on an occasional lap the bathroom, all the while proclaiming at the top of his voice, "Oh mummy and daddy, that's the best news! The best news I ever heard! I am going to have a wee brother!"

It never seemed to dawn on him that there was a 50 -50 chance the promised addition to the Arnold family could be "a wee sister." That possibility didn't even merit a thought!

When he had worked off the first phase of euphoria and was visibly beginning to 'run out of steam' his mum spoke to him again. What we have told you tonight is still a secret, son. So don't tell anybody in the meantime. What you can do, though, is pray to God that He will give us a healthy baby. Will you do that?"

"Yes, I will indeed," he promised before returning, reluctantly, to his bedroom.

That time he stayed in it,

As the months ticked by, Hertford and Phyllis thought and talked and prayed much about the baby to come.

The idea took some getting used to. After nine years they had become convinced they weren't going to be privileged to share their home and lives with any more children, and now this. They were going to have another one, a fourth.

Would he or she prove to be another blessing from the Lord, or a further test of their faith?

What if?

Chapter 32
MATTHEW

It was February, the very dead of winter, and cold and raw outside. Inside, though, in my study, it was warm and cosy, a comfortable atmosphere in which to share confidences.

Hertford and Phyllis had come to see me to do some further research into this book.

As we started to talk I noticed that they seemed rather on edge. They appeared restless. It came across as though they had something to say but weren't quite sure if, or how, to say it. This was unusual. Normally we had an open, friendly, trusting relationship.

Eventually Phyllis 'broke the ice.'

"Do you remember, Noel, you told us a while ago to think of a last chapter for the book?" she began, appearing to measure every word carefully. "You said you would like it to end on a high. 'With a bang, and not with a whimper,' was how you put it to us."

"Yes, I do. I remember," I replied. Deciding exactly where to end a biography is like deciding where to start it. It can be a problem sometimes.

"Well, we believe we have that last chapter for you now," she continued rather sheepishly.

"That's good. Where do you think we should end?" I enquired.

"Didn't you say you would like to have it finished by June?" Phyllis parried my question by asking one of her own.

"That's right," I had to agree. "I did say that."

My affirmation provided Phyllis with the cue she needed to continue, "We have news then that should give you an exciting last chapter to the book, no problem. You see we are expecting another baby in June."

There was an awkward silence for a moment.

This would take some thinking about, but I didn't have a lot of time to think. My two friends were sitting directly opposite me. The tension was gone, they had opened their hearts, and were now awaiting my reaction.

"That is some news!" I began, not very sure of just how to respond. "I must admit I am a bit shocked."

"A *bit* shocked are you?!" Hertford countered. "I will tell you this, you're not as shocked as I was!"

Then he smiled. Looking over to where I was sitting, pen poised, he quipped, "Noel, can you spell 'numb'?"

An animated conversation ensued, when Hertford and Phyllis, relieved that I now knew their 'secret', shared with me how they felt about the prospect of having a fourth child.

"We believe that this is the hand of God," Phyllis stated. "This is God's way of showing His approval for this book project. His timing is, as always, spot on."

"Yes," Hertford added. "Whatever happens, you will definitely have an end for the book."

'Whatever happens' had replaced the 'what if?' of earlier days.

Spring, with its daffodils in the lane, and lambs in the field, seemed to fly past, largely unnoticed, in flashes of yellow and bouncing bundles of white. Hertford and Phyllis were still very busy and every spare moment was spent in thinking about, and planning for, the new baby.

It wasn't long until their 'secret' could be 'kept a secret' no longer.

Mums and dads were the first to be told the good news.

Then other close relatives were informed. When the news was released to their wider circle of acquaintances the whole countryside was abuzz with it.

Friends speaking to Hertford and Phyllis congratulated them outwardly and told them they were 'so happy' for them and that it was 'great'. Inwardly, though, they just hoped and prayed the young couple wouldn't be heartbroken again.

The parents to-be prayed much themselves, too, during those days, and found it difficult. "Lord, we want Your will to be done in our lives," they would begin. "We know this new baby is from Youself." Then there was always the temptation to add, "And please God let him or her be normal."

June came. All would be revealed in a matter of days. 'What if?' was soon to become 'What now?'

On the thirteenth of the month at 10.20am the new baby arrived.

It was a boy. He weighed six pounds and half-an-ounce and had red hair, just like his dad.

What a relief! At least he had arrived safely!

Following the birth there was an anxious wait while tests were carried out.

It didn't take long and the results were marvellous. The hospital doctors were pleased to assure Hertford and Phyllis that their fourth son was a perfectly normal and healthy baby boy!

What excitement! What praise! What a wonderful caring God they had!

Phyllis was absolutely drained, and unbelievably delighted.

Ford was absolutely ecstatic and unbelievably excited.

Hertford was just a wonderful mixture of every pleasant emotion known to man.

Soon the flowers, presents and cards began to arrive at the hospital.

Soon family and friends began to arrive at the hospital. The delighted grandparents were among the first to appear, followed closely by the new baby's aunts, uncles and cousins galore. Then interested friends from near and far showed up to meet this latest addition to the Arnold family.

"And what are you going to call him?" seemed one of the most obvious questions to ask, so most of the visitors asked it, as they admired the miniature perfection of his little hands and feet, his tiny fingers and toes.

The baby yawned and stretched and slept and ignored everybody!

"We are calling him Matthew," his happy parents were delighted to inform all enquirers. "We have chosen this name because Matthew means 'a gift from God', and that is what he is to us, our gift from God.

On Sunday 18th June, 1995, Hertford and Ford arrived at the hospital to bring Phyllis and Matthew home. They made several return journeys between car and ward until they had all the flowers and presents safely packed into the car.

Then came the big moment. The four of them were united as a happy family, driving home.

On arrival at their bungalow Phyllis sat in the car with baby Matthew. Dad and big brother carried the presents, flowers and cards into the house and left them in what had once been Thomas and Wendsley's room.

Then Phyllis gently carried their new baby, their fourth son, into the bungalow and laid him in a pram in that room.

The rainbows and clouds, balloons and teddies which had once delighted earlier occupants, surrounded him.

It had been Thomas and Wendsley's room once, but God, in His grace and wisdom had other plans for it.

It is Matthew's room now.

He is their latest 'gift from God.'

2012 UPDATE

Chapter 33
BUY THE FIELD FOR MONEY

Matthew's homecoming was a tremendous climax to months of prayer and speculation. It was like sunshine after rain, a case of happiness after pain.

Hertford and Phyllis now had two sons. They wouldn't occupy every place at the long kitchen table, but there would at least be the sound of an infant laughing and crying, followed by a toddler walking and talking, in the bungalow once more.

Ford had the 'wee brother' he had asked for, and his mum and dad had been blessed with a 'gift from God.'

As the boys developed, week by week, then month by month, so did the business in 'the jelly house' up the yard. Orders were pouring in to Cottage Catering, with new customers being added every month. Hertford and Phyllis employed additional staff to help cope with the demand, but despite long hours and hard work it was becoming increasingly difficult to fulfil their orders on time. The problem was neither a lack of dedication by the workforce nor ingredients for their desserts. It was a lack of space. They needed to install more machinery but had nowhere to put it!

One day as Hertford and Phyllis were driving through Dromore they noticed a sign at the edge of a large field. It read, 'Individual sites for sale.' Both agreed that if they could buy a sizeable site in that location they could possibly build a factory and install more, and also more modern, machinery.

It would be worth investigating.

They phoned the agent and went to see him on a Thursday afternoon in the autumn of 1995. He showed them a map of the site which had been passed for development. Hertford and Phyllis reckoned it would be ideal for the expansion plans they felt forced to consider.

The agreement was they were to take the weekend to 'think it over' and return the following Tuesday to sign the contract.

'Thinking it over' was to include more than merely 'thinking it over'. It was to include a lot of 'talking it over' and much 'praying it over'.

They had to consider that if they moved to a purpose built factory in Dromore then 'Cottage Catering' would no longer be a home industry.

Such a move was going to involve extraordinary expense. Would God want them to spend that amount of money?

On the other hand, was it not God who had blessed them thus far? And if He had done that and they had given, and were giving all the glory to Him, would it not be right to develop even further?

There was a lot to 'think over'.

Early on Tuesday morning Hertford, who had been having his daily 'quiet time' in the kitchen called to his wife, who was in the bedroom, preparing to go and meet the agent, "Hi Phyllis, come up to you hear this."

When she arrived beside him, where he sat in an armchair by the Aga, Phyllis found Hertford with the UCB Word for Today, and the Bible, both on his knee.

"I just couldn't believe it," her husband began, having instructed her to 'sit down a minute'.

"I was reading the notes there and discovered this verse. I had never heard it before, and didn't even know it was in the Bible, so I looked it up. Listen to this. It is in Jeremiah chapter 32 and it's verse 25. 'Thou hast said unto me, O Lord God, Buy thee the field for money, and take witnesses.' That verse just jumped out at me when I read it. Buy the field for money. That's it!"

Phyllis leant forward. She wanted to see it in the Bible as well. When she had assured herself that it was definitely 'in the Book,' she felt as though the cloud of indecision had mysteriously vanished.

God had said it, they would do it. Buy the field for money.

The agent, though, when they called for their appointment, to agree a price and sign the contract, had other ideas. He was just about to 'throw a spanner in the works.'

"I have been thinking that if you buy the field at the front you are negotiating for, that means I will have no access to the smaller field behind and I could sell a lot of sites on it for private housing," he said.

It appeared to Hertford and Phyllis as if he were about to renege on the deal. They were not to be deterred, however, and each of them was prepared to voice an opinion on all the 'ifs' and 'buts' the agent was raising.

"It's funny you never mentioned that when we were talking last week," Hertford remarked, before going on to suggest a solution. "But I tell you what we'll do. There is a way to get round it. We will buy both fields from you!"

That unexpected offer gave the agent something different to consider before Phyllis followed up with, "The way I look at it is this. If God wants us to be here, neither you, nor me, nor anybody else will stop it!"

They then set about negotiating a price for both fields and Hertford and Phyllis left. This time it was the agent who asked for some time to 'think it over.'

He didn't take long about it, either. He had obviously been influenced by the enterprising couple's enthusiasm and offer, plus the fact they appeared to have God on their side somehow. Next morning he was on the phone to say he would be happy to let them have the two fields for the price agreed.

There followed a period of planning, and with more land than they had originally expected at their disposal, Hertford and Phyllis decided to build a slightly larger factory than they had at first thought.

Construction work began on 3rd January 1996, and the new owners made frequent visits to the site in spring and early summer. They were watching the building take shape, involved in discussions about minor alterations which they felt would improve either the appearance or efficiency of the manufacturing unit to come, and then eventually the supervision of all the original plant from their bungalow in Donacloney to their factory in Dromore.

Hertford and Phyllis took over their new premises in mid-August and on the night before they were due to bring the staff in to start work in it they stopped a few minutes to survey what they had planned to be their production floor.

The couple stood in one corner of it, looking diagonally across at the machines huddled as though afraid of something, in the far corner. They seemed so far away, and there was so much echoing emptiness all around them. Phyllis thought it looked just like an airport hangar minus its aeroplanes.

She was suddenly overtaken by a tremor of trepidation.

"This place is so big!" she exclaimed, unable to contain herself any longer. "We have spoiled the family homeliness of the whole thing, too. What have we done, Hertford? What have WE done?!"

"I'm a bit scared too," her husband had to confess. Not willing, though, to reveal just how anxious he was, he went on to try and reassure both of them by refreshing their minds of God's goodness and guidance. "Sure we believe it was God who directed us to this site and this size. And anyway, Phyllis, do you not remember what we heard in a meeting, I'm not sure where it was, a while ago? Not remember it? The preacher told us there are 366 'Fear not' promises in the Bible, one for every day of the year,"

"I think I do, now that you mention it," Phyllis replied. "And I can tell you, we are going to need them all!"

With that they both laughed, and went home to prepare for welcoming the staff to their positions on a much smoother and more efficient production line the next morning.

When the factory was fully operational, and with any minor 'teething troubles' corrected, it was time for the official opening of Cottage Catering on its Dromore site.

The opening ceremony was performed by Baroness Denton, and the crowd of family and friends, plus local dignitaries and businessmen were given a conducted tour of the factory by the staff.

With the tour over it was the turn of Phyllis to thank everyone for coming and to give a brief but poignant history of the company up until that date.

No one could fail to notice the close family connections to the business, as Phyllis made her speech. Having thanked Baroness Denton for coming that day, and all those involved with the planning and construction of the building in which they stood, as well as their current employees, she focused on the family.

Phyllis thanked Hertford's parents, Ford and Jean, for looking after the boys in the early days, and so allowing them to carry on with the work

She thanked her own father, Tom, for driving the delivery lorry, and her sisters Heather and Gloria who had been with them 'since the very beginning' and her brother Linden who had recently joined the staff.

Having mentioned everyone she could think of except the two key players, Phyllis went on to add, "It may not ring a bell with you but today is the 12th of November. That means it is exactly seven years ago today since our son Thomas was taken into hospital suffering from a chest infection, but he didn't come out. He died two days later.

It was for him, and for his younger brother Wendsley that I started making trifles, for they found them easy to eat, and loved them. It is to the memory of them that Hertford and I would like to dedicate this factory. They will never be forgotten."

There were people in that audience who knew the story as Phyllis told it, and others, including businessmen and sales reps, who had never heard it before.

It had the same effect on all.

Everyone was touched. Women wept, and men tried to hold back tears.

Phyllis still hadn't finished. She had just one more thing to say. It involved someone else who had to be thanked.

"I am almost finished, but before I sit down I would like to thank the Lord for all He has done for us, and how He has guided in our lives and brought us to where we are now. All praise and glory must go to Him, and it is in Him we are trusting as we carry on this business into the future," she declared.

It was a clear testimony to the faith both Hertford and she had in God, and seemed, to the many Christians present, like a wise move to incorporate Him in all their forward planning.

Chapter 34
GOING BACK TO YOUR ROOTS

"We are going to have to put our toe in the water here, Hertford," Phyllis remarked to her husband one afternoon in the factory. "We will have to try and tap into the major supermarket chains across the water."

It was 1999 and they were measuring their manufacturing capacity against actual output and current sales figures. After the factory had been open for a while they had reckoned it unprofitable to have so much potential production space lying empty, and so had purchased more machinery and employed further staff.

So far it had been going well. Lorries were leaving Cottage Catering in Dromore and delivering desserts to destinations all over the island of Ireland, and many convenience stores in Scotland.

Hertford recognised that putting his 'toe in the water' would involve more than going for a paddle in the sea at Newcastle. He knew what Phyllis meant, and she was right. If they could win over some larger customers they could manufacture to optimum capacity.

They had a good product, and the only way to expand sales was to pitch it to the major grocery retailers. The most effective way to achieve this goal, they agreed, was to apply to become an exhibitor at some of the main shows for the food trade. This would allow them to showcase the quality and variety of their desserts to a much wider prospective market.

Contacts were made and the appropriate applications sent

off and for the next few years Cottage Catering had a stand at wholesale food shows in large mainland venues, such as Earls Court in London and the NEC in Birmingham.

It proved a rewarding move. Hertford and Phyllis and those manning their exhibits were successful in obtaining substantial orders from some of the larger grocery chains.

Now they could use all the space in their Dromore factory to its fullest extent, and there were soon three lorries leaving the factory every day to deliver all over Great Britain and Ireland.

With all this expansion, Hertford and Phyllis never forgot how it began, who it had been originally for, and Who had helped them through the previous twelve to fifteen years. In more reflective moments Phyllis would stop at some point in what were becoming increasingly hectic days, and say to her husband, "Can you ever believe, Hertford how this all started, back in the kitchen at Donacloney? Me making trifles for Thomas and Wendsley, our two handicapped sons who crowed when they saw them coming, for they were so tasty and easy to eat. It was totally of God. It had to be God. It was nothing else!"

In addition to her love for the Lord, and her husband and family, Phyllis's other passion was for animals. She had been reared having dogs, cats and all kinds of pet and animal life around her, so it was no surprise to anyone who knew her that she was 'on the lookout,' as she described it, for another dog.

As part of her quest she bought the 'Belfast Telegraph' on her way home from Dromore to Donacloney one Thursday evening in June 2003. When the two boys, Ford and Matthew, had retired to their bedrooms, but perhaps not yet to bed, later on that night, Phyllis lifted her paper with the intention of scanning the ads pages to see if there were any dogs she fancied advertised in the 'Pets' column.

As she opened the newspaper, however, the 'Homefinder' insert fell out onto the floor at her feet. Picking it up either to be cast aside or shoved back between the centre pages, her attention was attracted to the property featured on the front of the section.

It was Killaney Lodge, a country residence in County Down, and a property she had often admired when driving past on business or to speak at an evening engagement somewhere. As far as Phyllis was concerned this wasn't just any old house for sale.

She knew the history of the place and the family who had lived there for generations, plus the current occupants. There was a nostalgic attraction as well. The 'Homefinder' description of Killaney Lodge reminded her so forcibly of Grace Hall, the country home in which she had lived so happily as a Blakely daughter and sister.

By the time Hertford appeared in the kitchen where she was sitting, Phyllis had completely forgotten that it was a dog she wanted. "Guess what, Hertford," she began enthusiastically, "but Killaney Lodge is for sale. It's on the front page of that 'Homefinder' thing in the 'Tele.' It's a marvellous place. Do you know it?"

"Of course I know it," her husband was quick to respond. "But have a bit of sense, Phyllis. We could never buy a place like that!"

"I'm not talking about buying it, Hertford. But I really would love to see through yon place. I have always wanted to have a walk in the grounds of it," Phyllis told him before going on, "Is it all right if I put on an appointment with the agent to go and see it? Just for a laugh, you know."

"Aye, go ahead if you like," Hertford said, before dismissing the prospect of a visit to Killaney Lodge as just another Phyllis fantasy.

His wife wasted no time, though. She called the agent next day and arranged for them to see around 'this desirable residence' the following Tuesday, 17th June.

It was a beautiful summer day when Hertford and Phyllis were first introduced to the property. They were given a conducted tour of the house and outbuildings before taking some free time to explore the large and obviously carefully planned and maintained garden.

As they were passing the garden pool and heading back towards the house where the owner and agent were both awaiting their return, Hertford said, with the same measure of enthusiasm as his wife had used when reading him the ad, just six days earlier, "I'm going to give this a go, ma!"

Phyllis was surprised at the ardour of that outburst and it caused her to sound a note of caution. It had come her turn to take charge of the cold water bucket, and she felt it was time to pour some of its contents on his impulsive proposal.

"Catch yourself on, Hertford!" she replied at once. "You have lived in Donacloney all your life, and you are talking about coming over here. It would break your mother and father's hearts if we and the boys weren't about in the yard!"

It was a consideration, but not a defining or conclusive one, as far as Hertford was concerned. He was hooked on Killaney Lodge, and Phyllis had to confess she was as well.

In an attempt to obtain another opinion Hertford and Phyllis decided to arrange for their son Ford, who had just completed his A levels in Banbridge Academy, to view the house and grounds.

When they did, and he had seen not only the house but also the space and animal pens outside, his reaction was emphatic, brief and totally positive.

"Da, go for it!" was his terse recommendation.

It was the encouragement his parents needed, and

confident that eight-year old Matthew would be happy to live in a house with such a potential for outdoor fun around it, they considered, then presented, an initial offer.

They were by then quite excited about the possibility of moving to a new home but Phyllis had one niggling reservation. Hertford's parents were in their seventies and if their son and his wife and family moved away from 'the home place' they might not be pleased.

She voiced her concern one evening, saying to Hertford as they stood in the bungalow kitchen, "We will have to tell your mother and father about this soon, before news of it gets out, through the boys or something. How are we going to break the ice, though?" she wondered.

"The best thing to do would be to take ma and da over there and let them see it," he replied, well aware that it had to be done. "We will go over and ask if they would like to go across to see Killaney Lodge."

This was a dramatic decision for Hertford, and he was afraid of what his mum and dad would say when they heard this news. Would they even bother to go with them for a viewing session? He was so nervous that he told Phyllis on the way over to his parents' house, "I haven't a spit left in my mouth and yet the water's running off my hands!"

When they carried out phase one of their plan, and were standing with Ford (senior) Arnold and his wife in the farm kitchen, Hertford asked, "Tell me, ma and da, are you doing anything tonight the pair of you?"

His parents looked across at each other and shook their heads. "No, we have nothing arranged. Why?" his mum replied.

"Well, you see, we are considering buying a place, and we would like you to come and have a look at it and hear what you think," their son told them.

Ford the father was puzzled. "A place. What kind of a place? Another factory or something like that?" he was anxious to know.

"Not a factory. It's a house over near Saintfield called Killaney Lodge and we have been to see it a couple of times." Hertford informed him.

"Killaney Lodge! I know it well!" his father exclaimed, then turning to his wife he said, "Jean, could you go into the good room and bring in the photo of the house where my grandfather lived?"

Jean duly returned with the said photo. It was of a group of people, women in black dresses and men in rough tweed suits and waistcoats, standing outside a whitewashed cottage. "That's where my granda lived," Ford told his mightily relieved son and daughter-in-law. "And that house is less than a mile from Killaney Lodge. If you go to live there, Hertford, you will simply be going back to your roots!"

Things had taken an unexpectedly pleasant turn and with feelings of relief mixed with virtual disbelief Hertford phoned the owner of Killaney Lodge and asked permission to bring his parents over for a viewing session. This was granted, and as the four of them were walking around the grounds after having had a tour of the house, men ahead, women behind, Jean said to the younger woman at her side, "This is a marvellous place, Phyllis. If I were your age I would definitely go for it!"

What an answer to prayer! Phyllis and Hertford had been praying for God's guidance in relation to this property deal, and they were prepared to accept the reaction of their family as an indicator of His will. With Ford and Jean's approval they felt as if the ice had not only been broken, but also that the iceberg from which it had come had simply melted and floated away!

With Phyllis' extended family also encouraging them to proceed, Hertford and Phyllis's entered into serious and often prayerful negotiations, to buy Killaney Lodge. It was a slow and often nerve-racking experience, but they believed that as with the field on which to build a factory, so also with this very attractive country house, if God wanted them to have it they would get it.

And they did. Their final bid was accepted and the sale agreed on 7th July, 2003.

The lady living in the house asked if it would be possible for them to delay taking possession of their new home until the spring. Hertford and Phyllis were happy to go along with this arrangement as it would give them the winter to prepare for the move.

That preparation included heartfelt thanksgiving to God for allowing them to purchase such a spacious home coupled with a commitment to find a way to use it for His glory.

Such was the grace and kindness of God too, that the home, to which they believed He had led them, came with three bonus points.

It turned out that the former owner was concerned about her much-loved pets. "I am moving to live in the Isle of Man," she explained, in one of their meetings prior to the big change-over, "and I cannot take my dogs with me. Would you be willing to keep them here? I look on this as their home and I'm sure so do they."

Hertford and Phyllis were amazed at this offer and delighted to say "Yes."

So it was that when they moved into their country residence on Friday 27th February, 2004, there were three dogs waiting for them in the yard. Phyllis, who had gone on 'the look-out for a dog' less than a year before had acquired three of them all at once.

Killaney Lodge had come with Monty and Holly the Labradors and Henry the big Rhodesian Ridgeback as part of the package!

Chapter 35
JOB DONE

During the spring and summer of 2004 Hertford and Phyllis hosted at least three 'house warming parties' every week. These could either be arranged or impromptu. With the new owners of Killaney Lodge each being members of large families there were plenty of brothers and sisters, in-laws, cousins, nephews and nieces, all anxious to see 'the place Hertford and Phyllis have bought.'

There were very few days that there wasn't somebody calling, often with a present, to wish them every blessing in their new home.

One of the novelty attractions, particularly for the younger visitors, was what had developed over the summer months into a sort of pet zoo. With all the stables and paddocks they had inherited, Phyllis and Hertford added to the resident animals left behind by the former owner. This meant that when it came to July they had Shetland ponies, a Highland cow, pot-bellied pigs, a number of donkeys, a variety of rare hens, ducks and geese and two alpacas all down the yard.

The alpacas were Matthew's special pets, and his party-piece, performed for admiring cousins of all ages, was to have one of them eat its food from his hand.

Sunday afternoons were always very busy at Killaney Lodge. Relatives and friends who were 'just out for a wee run' often called in to see Hertford and Phyllis, Ford and Matthew. Neither mum and dad nor the two boys could ever be sure whether it was them as people, or the house and garden, or the menagerie in the adjoining stables and paddocks, that was the main motive for their unscheduled visit, but it didn't matter.

If God had led Hertford and Phyllis to purchase this house then they reckoned they ought to be prepared to welcome His children into it at any time.

It was on one of those bustling Sunday afternoons, with friends calling, laughing, meeting and mixing that Phyllis noticed something unusual. She was the only one to spot it, and it worried her.

There was a group of ten people of all ages standing looking into a pen at Molly, the Highland cow. They were talking away, pointing and asking questions. With everybody engrossed in conversation, Ethel, Phyllis's mum, slipped away from the crowd and started walking slowly up the slight incline towards the house.

This wasn't like Ethel Blakely. She usually loved to be involved in all that was going on, especially when her children and grandchildren were around. Concerned that something may have upset her, or that she was finding the heat overpowering, for it was a very warm day, Phyllis excused herself from the others and followed her.

She caught up with her mum just before they both reached the house, and asked immediately, "Mummy, are you all right?"

"Don't worry, Phyllis, I'll be OK," Mother replied. "I have a bit of a headache and I'm going up to get a couple of Anadins out of my handbag."

They went into the kitchen and Phyllis poured her mum a drink of water, she took her tablets and they chatted. Soon others started to filter back into the house and as Phyllis began attending to them her mum disappeared again.

This was definitely strange. Having looked in a few of the rooms Phyllis found her eventually in the dining room, surveying the furniture and ornaments. She looked well, in her powder blue summer suit, her daughter thought, but there was a curiously strained look on her face.

Aware that she was no longer alone, Ethel said, "This is some place you have here, Phyllis. I hope and pray that Hertford and you will have many years of health and happiness in it, with the boys. I love it for it reminds me so much of Grace Hall."

Phyllis thanked her mum for her sincere good wishes and then they headed back up into the buzz of the kitchen where a few adults were sitting around talking. The children weren't to be seen. They were all either involved in intense conversation or excited exploration outside, according to age.

Ethel didn't want to stay much longer, and soon she and her husband were on their way out to the car. When they were about to drive off, Phyllis called to them in through the rolled down windows, "I'll not stand at the door to wave, for I have to go inside and open the gates to let you out."

"No you don't, dear," her mum called back, "We have our own wee zapper thing here." Then just to prove the point she held up the remote control Phyllis had given her, and promptly forgotten about, soon after they had moved in.

As she watched her parents' car disappear down the drive and out of the gate, Phyllis remarked to Hertford, "Wouldn't it be awful if anything happened to mummy or daddy?"

It proved to be a strange premonition.

Two days later, on Tuesday at lunch time, Phyllis had a phone call from Estlin, one of her brothers. He told her of a devastating discovery made by another brother. "Alva has found mummy lying on the kitchen floor, unconscious, with Basil, her wee Jack Russell, lying across her legs," he said.

Phyllis wasted no time. She was almost numb with shock but still had the presence of mind to get into the car and drive to her mummy's house. Hers was one of a number of vehicles arriving into the yard 'at home' in quick succession. Soon husband Tom plus all seven of Ethel Blakeley's sons and daughters had gathered, desperately worried, and keen to hear the latest news.

The ambulance was there also, and soon their father was heading off in it, with his unconscious wife, to Craigavon Hospital.

Family members followed in their cars and waited around anxiously, a sense of disbelief allowing them to communicate only in clipped sentences. There was no small talk. Their mum was in Intensive Care, obviously seriously ill. Conversation about any other subject seemed irrelevant, almost irreverent.

Everyone's worst fears were confirmed when a consultant spoke to them later. "Mrs. Blakely has suffered a brain haemorrhage, and is gravely ill," he told them. "We will be keeping her in the Intensive Care Unit and monitoring her condition overnight."

A few days later Phyllis's mum was moved out of Intensive Care and on to another ward. She was beyond medical intervention. It was, the doctors said, "Just a matter of time."

The large, loving and caring family then began taking it in turns to maintain a bedside vigil, with their dad, Tom, who was there most of the time.

One night, after 11pm Phyllis was sitting on one side of the bed and her dad on the other. This gave her the opportunity to speak to him one-to-one about something which had long been worrying her and the lady whom they both loved, and who was now lying, neither hearing nor speaking, between them.

It would, she reckoned, be most easily presented in the form of a story.

Tom had done his fair share of reminiscing over the

last few days. As he sat there holding Ethel's hand Phyllis recalled another memory she knew he would find interesting. Recounting this particular incident from the recent past allowed her to introduce her subject. "I must tell you, daddy, about a couple of chats I had with mummy one day in June past," she began.

"I took a meeting in Limavady one night then called to take her out shopping the next morning. Before we left the house mummy made a cup of tea and as we were talking together about all sorts of things over it she asked me, "Did you see anybody you knew at your meeting last night?"

"I told her I didn't but there was a good crowd at it. A few of them seemed to be touched by what I had to say, but I would be worried about some of the rest of them. They were elderly and appeared set in their ways, but with no interest in either God or their future destiny.

"Then I spoke to her directly and said, "Not like you mummy. If anything happens to you I'll know where you are."

"When I said that she replied with great confidence, "I might not be like you, Phyllis, out taking meetings two or three times a week, but I love the Lord Jesus Christ and I have Him in my heart. It's not me you have to worry about. It's your father. Whatever is it going to take to speak to him?"

Choosing then to press home the point she had set out to make, Phyllis went on, "You know better than anybody, daddy, what Hertford and I have been through in our lives. In fact the both of you lived through every agonising minute of it with us. So I told her, "Maybe God will have to take the most precious thing daddy loves away, to make him look up, the way he had to do with Hertford and me."

Tom Blakely was gazing at the figure in the bed. She hadn't moved, and she wasn't going to move. He knew the process had already started. His Ethel's life was ebbing away.

Aware of, but choosing not to comment on, his loving look, his daughter continued, "We had finished our tea by that time so we pushed our chairs under the table and went out into the car to go shopping in Lisburn. As we were driving down to the Moira roundabout mummy said, out of the blue, "You'll never guess what I got in the post this morning, Phyllis. Our grave tickets. If you go right round the roundabout and back up to the Parish Church I would like to show you where our burying ground is."

"That was one thing I wasn't prepared to do, as you can guess. I didn't even want to think of either of you in a grave, so I said, "You know, mummy, I would drive you to the ends of the earth if I thought you needed to go there. But that's one place to which I definitely don't want to go. Your grave."

The look on her dad's face showed Phyllis he was totally gripped by this round of story-telling. This inspired her to carry on, "As we drove on towards Lisburn mummy laughed and said, "I'm sure you think I'm mad, the way I get on. We had a choice. There was a plot near the hedge or one beside the drive. So we decided to go for the one near the drive, so you children can pull up in the cars if it's raining. You won't even have to get out of the car."

Nodding down at her motionless mum, as though to somehow gain her approval for the next stage, Phyllis added, "I've been wondering the last few days if she knew something like this was going to happen. She can't speak to us now, but I'm sure mummy would want me to say this to you for her. You will have to make an important decision, daddy. You have loved her so much all your life. Wouldn't it be nice to say that one day you will meet her again in heaven?"

"Yes. It would indeed," Tom agreed, obviously trying to avoid becoming too emotional. That statement ended the conversation. There was little left to say.

Having done all she could to make her dad aware of her

deep concern for him, Phyllis committed her father to God, praying that He would intervene in his life. The answer to that prayer came two days later.

Ethel's brother Eddie asked John Purcell, an itinerant evangelist, if he would call and pray with the Blakely family the next time he was visiting in Craigavon Hospital. He did so, and after he had been to the ward and prayed with those present, some of them accompanied John down to the entrance hall where they had coffee together.

After spending some time in general conversation, the family members gradually dispersed, some to go home and others to resume the bedside vigil. This left Tom Blakely alone with John Purcell. Recognising this as a God-given opportunity, John explained the way of salvation to the anxious husband and led him to faith in Christ.

Phyllis met her dad in a corridor of the hospital when she arrived for an evening sit at her mum's bedside, and asked, "How did you get on with John when you were talking to him earlier?"

His response sent a wave of joy flooding over his daughter's heart. "You don't have to worry about me now, Phyllis. I've got that wee job done. If anything happens to your mummy I'll see her again in heaven," he declared.

There were tears in both their eyes as Phyllis hugged her daddy and exclaimed, "It's a wee job you'll never regret."

His simple expression of assured faith and his daughter's unbridled delight in recognising what it meant for both time and eternity, made the parting just slightly more bearable when the treasured wife and mother passed into the presence of the Lord, less than a week later, on Monday, 30th August.

She had gone to heaven to be with the Saviour she had loved so long when on earth.

With 'that wee job done' Tom will join them in due course.

Chapter 36
NO SMOKE WITHOUT FIRE

In late January 2010 Norrie Emerson held a week of meetings on prophetic subjects in Ardmore Gospel Hall. Hertford and Phyllis were interested in the topical subjects he was addressing from the Bible, and attended as many nights as they possibly could.

Friday 29th January was to be the last night of the series and during that day Phyllis phoned her brothers Alva and Estlin who both promised to go with Hertford and her to hear Norrie's message. When they left home, Ford and his girlfriend Nicola were watching TV but Hertford and Phyllis brought Matthew with them. He was looking forward to having a 'sleep-over' with Estlin and Debbie's two sons, Adam and Ryan.

On the way to the Gospel Hall on the shores of Lough Neagh the couple collected Phyllis's two brothers and left Matthew off with his cousins. They went to the meeting and afterwards Alva had a call from Jackson, another of the Blakely brothers, inviting them all round to his house for supper.

This invitation was gratefully accepted and the chat was good. Time passed quickly and it was after midnight before the party broke up with Hertford and Phyllis still having Alva and Estlin to leave off on their way home.

When they reached their house the electric gates opened, as usual, at the push of the remote button. On driving up into the courtyard, however, Phyllis noticed something unusual.

The electric clock in the courtyard had stopped.

When they went out any evening it was customary to leave a few table lamps on in different rooms around the house, just to give the place 'a lived in' look. They weren't on that night. The house was in total darkness.

It was a clear starry night, and a brilliant moon shed the only light on an otherwise pitch black scene.

Hertford stated the obvious before even getting out of the car. "There must be a power cut," he said.

There was more than a power cut, though.

Phyllis was first to step out into the courtyard and as soon as her feet touched the ground she asked anxiously, "Hertford, do you smell smoke?"

It was a question her husband didn't need to answer. Thick black smoke was billowing out of a chimney they had never used in the previous six years, and possibly the former owners had seldom, if ever, used either.

Hertford pushed open the back door and a cloud of smoke belched out round him, then past him and up into the winter night.

The message of the smoke was unmistakeable. Their house was on fire!

Phyllis began yelling, "Ford! Ford! Where are you, Ford?"

Her husband recognised that standing squealing may have been a natural and maternal reaction to the situation, but as far as he was concerned it required urgent action. After hastily grabbing a coat out of the car, then pulling it round his head and over his mouth, he disappeared into the blackness.

Phyllis was then left alone in the eerie stillness of a starlit night, watching black smoke pouring out of the back door. She went into hysterics.

Dashing round to below Ford's bedroom window she called out, "Ford! Ford! Ford!" The only response was an echo that seemed to travel for miles around and then come bouncing back to haunt her.

In desperation she clawed handfuls of soil and decorative stones out of a nearby flowerpot and began throwing them wildly up at the window.

No face appeared. There was no sign of life, no ray of hope. The sole response was the continued sinister smoke-scented silence.

Had her husband and eldest son both been burned alive? Or were they lying unconscious somewhere in the building, overcome by smoke and waiting for the flames to find them?

The prospect was horrendous and unthinkable.

Not that Phyllis was thinking about anything by then. Panic had replaced reason in her whirling mind, and it was panic which sent her running round towards the back door once more.

She didn't know what she was going to do, but was so grateful she didn't have any further decision to make. Just as she entered the courtyard and was crossing towards the door Hertford emerged from it, leading Ford. They were both bent double. Frightened eyes stared out of blackened faces.

Father and son fell to the ground, choking and coughing, fighting for breath.

"Praise the Lord you are both safe!" Phyllis screamed with joy and relief.

As soon as Hertford recovered sufficient breath to utter a sentence he asked urgently, "Have you rung the Fire Brigade, Phyllis?"

"No, I haven't," his worked up wife replied. "All I could think about was you and Ford. Anyway, come to think of it, how could I? We left both our phones charging on the island in the kitchen."

"That's not a problem," Hertford told her. "It'll not take me long getting in there."

With that he lifted the coat from where he had abandoned it following his initial rescue mission, and before Phyllis could even think of shouting a word of caution, he disappeared into the blackness for a second time.

He was right. It didn't take him long to locate the phones and he was out again with them inside a minute.

Handing Phyllis hers he said, "Ring 999."

Thankfully the phone worked and when an operator asked, "Which service please?" Phyllis shouted, "The Fire Brigade. Our house is on fire!"

"Who is calling, and what's the address where the fire is located?" was the measured response from the operator.

"It's Phyllis – Mrs. Phyllis Arnold," the distraught wife and mother was able to say, and then she forgot the address. There was a momentary pause until she gathered her thoughts before going on in a strangely high-pitched voice, "It's Killaney Lodge. You know on the road between Carryduff and Ballynahinch."

"Thank you, Mrs Arnold. We will have an appliance with you as soon as possible." The operator's tone was reassuring.

With everything sorted except the fire, Hertford ran down the drive to open the gates manually for the Fire Brigade, and Phyllis phoned her brother Estlin, whom they had left off just over an hour earlier. He told her that he would be over as soon as he could, and he would probably bring 'some of the other boys' as well.

In what seemed ages, but really was not all that long, the wail of the fire engine siren could be heard in the distance. It was on its way out from Ballynahinch at top speed. Hertford was at the gate to signal them in, and they were soon followed up to the front of the house by Alva, Estlin and Jackson who had arrived from the opposite direction. They hadn't wasted any time on the way either.

Phyllis calmed down slightly with all this help at hand. The firemen had jumped down from the fire engine and were donning their masks and oxygen tanks when one of them looked across at Phyllis and enquired, "What about the wee lad with the ginger hair? Where is he?"

This man had obviously noticed that there was only three-quarters of the Arnold family out in the courtyard. He was later to explain that he was the driver of the school bus which dropped Matthew off at the front gate every day. He and the fourteen-year old had often exchanged 'a bit of banter' on the bus.

Where was he now, though?

"Don't worry about Matthew," Phyllis told him. "He is spending the night at his cousin's house. There's nobody in there."

The Chief Fire Officer came across to where they were standing. "Could you give me a rough idea of the layout of the house, Mrs. Arnold?" he asked.

Phyllis did so, as best her befuddled mind would allow, and after he was sure he understood her brief explanation he made towards the back door to lead his team in.

He wasn't going to be allowed to get on with the main business of the night that quickly, however. Phyllis followed him, three or four paces behind. The once worried wife and mother was by then transformed into the worried homemaker. Aware of all the curtains, carpets and furniture she had chosen with great care in the previous six years, she had a last request to make. It sounded rather ridiculous, to all within earshot, but it meant a lot to her.

"Please don't use the water unless you have to," she begged.

"We will be doing all we can to locate the source of this fire and put it out," the officer replied.

His patience was no doubt wearing very thin. "Now Mrs.

Arnold would you please get back outside and stay outside," he went on to order. "You have no breathing apparatus and could be affected by smoke inhalation."

There was nothing more for it but to leave it to the experts. Hertford, Phyllis and Ford, plus Phyllis's three brothers all stood out in the courtyard or took occasional walks right out round the outside of house. All the windows were blackened by that time and one or two of them had cracked with the heat. What puzzled them was that there was thick choking smoke but they could never see flames anywhere.

The only lights to appear in the house were the beams of the lamps on the fire officers' helmets as they moved from room to room.

It didn't take them long to find the source of the problem. An electrical fault in 'the oak room' in one of the courtyard buildings had caused all the smoke, but the firemen dealt with it appropriately and soon brought it under control.

When they were satisfied that it was safe to leave, the crew began replacing all their equipment on the waiting fire engine. That was when the Chief Fire Officer told Hertford and Phyllis of a terrifying possibility.

"You people just came home at the very right time," he explained. "This fire burnt itself out for lack of air. But if you had come home any earlier and somebody had opened the door of that room up there when it was smouldering, it would have triggered an awful flashback. Whoever opened the door would never have survived, and the whole place would have been engulfed in flames within minutes."

Pausing for a second or two, and choosing to slightly lower his voice, he continued, "On the other hand if you had been much later, your son, who was asleep, could have been overcome by smoke."

"Thank God for that," Hertford replied instinctively. "This

could be nothing but the guidance of God."

When the fire engine eventually set off on its return journey to Ballynahinch, Hertford, Phyllis, Ford, Alva, Estlin and Jackson were free to re-enter the house. They were glad to be allowed inside once more after the chill of a January night, but the house was badly smoke damaged. Every room was affected.

With adrenalin pumping through their bodies not one of the three Killaney Lodge residents felt like going to bed, nor did the 'three boys' feel like going home. They stayed on and all did what they could, but it was hard to know where to start. Everything was smeared with sticky soot.

As Phyllis and Hertford moved from room to room surveying the damage they were gutted yet grateful. Every "Oh Hertford, this is dreadful!" was automatically followed by, "But it could have been worse. Three of us might not have been here today."

Hertford's reaction to his wife's anguish went something like, "It's bad looking sure enough, ma, but you're right. It could have been a lot worse. We will get this mess cleaned up sometime. But praise God we have been spared to do it!"

News of the fire spread fast. Soon after daybreak that winter Saturday morning relatives and friends began arriving at Killaney Lodge.

All who turned up had a statement to make and an offer to present. The initial declaration was on how 'lucky,' or for the more theological thinkers, how 'blessed,' the family were to be alive. The offer was a simple, "What can we do to help?"

Hertford's parents, Ford and Jean, called in the early afternoon. As soon as he came into the smoke-blackened residence granda Ford negotiated his way through the army of volunteers in aprons and overalls until he found grandson Ford.

Placing his arm round his grandson's shoulder and holding it there, Ford senior asked with a depth of sincerity that can only be generated by genuine love, "Are you all right, son? We could have lost you last night, you know."

When Ford the younger assured his concerned grandfather that he was indeed 'all right,' the old man was satisfied and free to focus his attention on his son and daughter-in-law.

Finding Hertford and Phyllis together for a brief moment in the midst of all that was going on around them he said, "Don't worry about the house, either of you. You'll soon have it all fixed up again. As long as nobody was hurt or killed, that's the main thing."

Late that afternoon another idea struck Phyllis. Watching all those who had come to help clear up the mess, still working away, she thought, "If we had perished in that fire all these loyal people would have been here arranging our funerals."

It was not the kind of thing she wanted to dwell on, so to dismiss it from her mind she switched to praising God for how they had all been preserved.

For perhaps the two hundredth time from 2am she repeated over and over again the three word phrase that came so readily to her lips.

It was, "Thank You, Lord! Thank You, Lord! Thank You, Lord! ..."

Chapter 37
THE MAN WITH TWO MOTHERS

Back in November 1996 when Phyllis made her moving speech at the opening of the new factory in Dromore she said they were trusting God as they planned the future of Cottage Catering.

Their trust was justified, and God honoured their public commitment to Him as the business expanded in the early years of the 21st century. What began as an experimental enterprise in a bungalow kitchen had long since outgrown its early Thomas and Wendsley-feeding beginnings. The appeal of it was that it never lost its intimate family feel.

This feeling increased even further when another member of the Arnold family joined the production team in Cottage Catering in the autumn of 2003.

Ford left Banbridge Academy that summer with four 'A' levels and was accepted to study electrical engineering at Queen's University, Belfast. He had only completed about six weeks of the first year, however, when he arrived home unexpectedly one afternoon.

Phyllis was surprised to see him and remarked, "You're home early today, son."

"Aye, I suppose I am," Ford conceded, before going on to enquire, "Where's da?"

"He's over at the factory, but why do you ask?" his mum was keen to know. She was a bit puzzled at this sudden interest in 'da'.

Setting a few books down on the island in the kitchen he

announced rather deliberately, "Well, I'm going there right now. Queen's wasn't all I thought it would be. I'm away to the factory."

He had neither sat down nor left his car keys down, and within seconds he was gone.

His dad was as surprised to see him arriving at the factory as his mum had been to see him arriving at the house, and said, "I thought you were at Queen's today. What are you doing here?"

"I was there today, you're right," Ford replied. "But Queen's is over for me. I'm not going back. I'm here to work."

Hertford raised no objections. He had never been the world's most enthusiastic student himself, so couldn't. What was more, business was expanding, and someone with Ford's knowledge of it, backed up by a wide range of capabilities, could prove invaluable in the days to come.

Ford didn't need a training course or an induction period. He simple changed his outdoor coat for a white factory coat and started to pack trifles. That was it! Cottage Catering had suddenly recruited its latest member of staff.

As he left teenage behind and progressed into his twenties, parallel developments took place in the life of Ford Arnold, junior. One of these related to his head, the other to his heart.

The heart matter concerned a girl he met, and with whom, after a very short time, he fell in love. Nicola Good and he just seemed to want to spend every moment they could spare with one another. She was the one he looked forward to seeing, or if that wasn't possible, certainly talking to, at some stage most days. It was pleasant, after a busy day at work, to have somebody in whom he could confide and with whom he could relax.

There were many hectic days in the factory, too. This was where Ford's head proved a valuable asset. After spending a short period on the production line, he moved up to the management team, with designated functions to perform. Initially he assumed the role of transport manager, organising the efficient delivery of orders. As time passed and he became more proficient in modern IT systems, he took charge of the computer division, handling both orders and accounts.

His presence was greatly appreciated as another pair of hands and another business mind, with orders continuing to stream in steadily. All the time Hertford and Phyllis spent attending trade shows in previous years was beginning to yield dividends.

Following the passing of Phyllis's mum in late August 2004 her dad, Tom, found his job driving a delivery lorry for Cottage Catering a tremendous source of both solace and fulfilment. There were at least three reasons for this.

Basically he had a job, something for which to get out of bed every morning. Secondly, he usually saw four of his own children every day. Phyllis, Heather, Gloria and Linden were all still there, performing vital roles in the management and production teams of the company. And finally, he couldn't avoid being reminded daily of the value of his newly-found faith.

The lorry he drove had a brief text painted across the back of it. As he approached the vehicle in the morning, or went round it ever so many times during the day's deliveries, he found the four-word message an inspiration, however difficult the day. 'Trust in the Lord' was the simple, yet spiritually rewarding course of action it recommended.

By 2009 the Cottage Catering factory floor, on which their single machine transported across from Donacloney had once looked so forlorn, was completely covered with fully automatic machinery. A staff of over 50 employees was busy turning out a product range of more than 30 chilled desserts.

The Dromore company's products were by then being dispatched to supermarket chains all over the UK mainland from Land's End to John O'Groats, as well as to existing customers on the island of Ireland. Their next move was to introduce the desserts, which had such homely beginnings, to the continental market. This proved satisfying for an unexpected reason. In 2011 Cottage Catering received the Product of the Year Award from a Dutch supermarket chain for their lemon cheesecake.

The constant demand for their popular desserts meant the factory had to operate a six-day week, worked in a shift pattern, and on occasions at busy periods 24-hour working was introduced.

At such pressure periods Hertford and Phyllis had another willing helper on whom they could call at short notice. He was their other son, Matthew.

The factory was a second home to Matthew as he was growing up. From the days shortly after they opened the new factory in Dromore when he spent hours in a large playpen in his mum's office, to the hours he spent there on Saturdays or in school holidays, he was familiar with every inch of the factory and its grounds.

Matthew gave his parents a lot of pleasure as he was growing up, as did Ford. Hertford and Phyllis were encouraged that Matthew had accepted Christ as Saviour at an early age and showed a growing interest in Christian activities during his teenage. They also knew he could be called upon to do a shift in the factory at any time, as he grew older.

Their son never complained about being called on when needed, for he had a goal in view. He was putting money aside for the car he was going to buy when he passed his driving test. By the time it came to June 2012 and his seventeenth birthday, Matthew was counting the days. He wanted to apply for his licence and the driving test so he could have his 'own wheels'.

A date was arranged for the driving test and Matthew passed it without any problem. This allowed him to fulfil the dream of years, to own his own car. He needed it too, for he had enrolled for an engineering course in Lisburn Further Education College. When this is complete he plans to join mum, dad and big brother in the factory in Dromore. Another person with technical skills would always be welcome there, with so much machinery to be maintained.

Meanwhile he has to continue working every Saturday to help with his expenses. He has discovered that after buying a car it costs money to keep it on the road!

Matthew 'shot up' during his teenage years and when he came seventeen was taller than Ford. Occasionally when they are together, and in relaxed mode, he reminds his brother of the fact. The bond between them is evident in the banter they exchange at such times.

"Don't worry about that, Ford," he would say, when his brother is reaching up for something above his head. "I'll get it down for you. Have you ever noticed that I'm taller than you now?"

"I have noticed actually," Ford would answer, "but does it matter? It's quality, not quantity that counts."

Keen to keep up the wisecracking, Matthew could continue with something like, "If you want to talk about quality then, has it ever struck you that I'm better looking as well?"

Ford is then left with only one option, and it is to deliver his knockout punch. "You think you're good looking do you, Matthew? But really you are still only a child. Never forget I'm a married man!"

In saying that he was reminding his younger, fun-loving brother of Friday 19 th August, 2011. That was the long-awaited blissful day when he married the love of his life,

Nicola, in Knock Methodist Church, Belfast. This was a happy occasion for both families. Nicola's great-uncle, Rev. Harold Good performed the wedding ceremony and Ford mentioned many members of the Arnold family in the course of his speech at the reception.

Having expressed his delight that Nicola had accepted his proposal of marriage, he went on to say, "I have a lot to be thankful for. I have parents who love me and catered for my every need in my youth. But in fact I have to explain that I'm not really like the rest of you here because I had two mothers. There was mother Phyllis who had me and the other was the mother who reared me when mum and dad were at work, Granny Jean.

"I must mention also my two brothers who are not able to be here today. Mum has a photo of Thomas and Wendsley on a table on the landing, just at the top of the stairs. I saw them every night before I went to bed. It would have been lovely to have them sitting here beside me today. I missed them so badly when they died. In fact I was so lonely and heartbroken I asked mum if I could have another wee brother for Christmas!

"She was patient with me and explained that baby brothers were not available in shops or by mail order, but perhaps God would allow me to have another brother in due course. He did, and I was absolutely thrilled. Then I woke up and saw what I'd got!

"Seriously, though, it's not as bad as that, really! Although there is a ten year difference in our ages Matthew and I have grown up to be best mates. Either I have become more tolerant or he has become more mature, I'm not sure which!"

Ford was to be reminded again of the circumstances of his early childhood, a few months after the wedding. It came in an unexpected way, in the form of a text message from America.

Suzie, whom Ford had known from schooldays, and her

husband Lee, who were then living in California were on a trip back to Northern Ireland She was visiting a friend of both Ford and herself one evening when she noticed a copy of the book 'Some Party in Heaven' on a shelf and asked if she could borrow it.

This was not a problem, and as her return flight from Dublin was delayed two hours she began reading the book in the airport and became totally engrossed in it. Once on the flight she was straight back into it, and before reaching her destination had read it all the way through.

Ford had a text from Suzie a few days later in which she told of reading 'Some Party in Heaven' on the flight. She said she had laughed at some parts of it and was in tears at others. The whole book she described as having been 'very moving.'

It was an apt description, not only of the book, but also of life for Hertford and Phyllis. There were times when they wondered if the trials were never-ending and yet they were able to come through, with the help and power of God, and the prayer support of hundreds of Christian friends. Some of these people they knew, others they didn't.

This is the testimony they have been giving both in meetings at home, and in churches and halls across Northern Ireland, for more than 17 years.

Having recognised that God had a purpose in leading them to Killaney Lodge, Phyllis started a monthly meeting for women in her home, commencing in the autumn of 2005. This continued monthly until 2010 when it had to be suspended for a year while the house was being refurbished after the fire.

The meeting is now up and running again and eagerly anticipated by all who attend. Hundreds of women, who are relatives, neighbours or friends of the family, have been challenged by the testimonies of the speakers invited to take part.

One of their speakers in 2012 was Sammy Graham from Ballynanhinch. He told Hertford and Phyllis of a woman he knew who had once been an alcoholic and had got saved. She read 'Some Party in Heaven' when it was first published in 1995, and although she had never met them in person, has been praying for them 'every single day' since.

When either Hertford or Phyllis separately, or both of them together, take a meeting anywhere and recount the story of how God moved them to come to Him through such a series of heartrending events, people are touched. There have been a number who have come to faith in Christ through hearing them speak or through reading the original version of this book, 'Some Party in Heaven.'

Perhaps the more frequent response to their testimony, however, is to hear of easygoing Christians who have been shaken out of their comfort zone, struggling Christians who have been strengthened in their faith, or backslidden Christians who have come back to close communion with God.

Hertford and Phyllis hear from or about many of these people but doubtless there are some who have no means of making contact. An example of a story which encouraged them occurred in September 2012. The couple attended a dinner held in Larchfield Estate outside Lisburn, and when they were on their way out to the car park after it finished a man approached Hertford.

"I didn't realise you would he here," he began, "but when I saw you I realised I must speak to you. I have been waiting for you to come out."

"That's OK friend, what can I do for you?" Hertford replied in his usual easy manner.

"I am coming from a very dark place. I thought I had problems in my life and was feeling very sorry for myself," the man explained. "Then I heard you speak at our church one night a few months ago and listened to what you and your wife had come through in your lives. That was when I discovered I didn't really have serious problems at all. The only thing I needed was a good kick up the backside, and your message gave it to me!"

Thus it is with Hertford and Phyllis. God has blessed them in their lives, and as He has blessed them, so they are constantly seeking to pass something of that blessing on to others. Like Paul in the Bible, they keep pressing 'toward the mark for the prize of the high calling of God in Christ Jesus'. (Phil.3:14)

They continue to set targets, and achieve goals. Whether in their business lives, spiritual lives or family lives there is always something up ahead which urges them to look forward.

Their furthest goal, and one for which they have already made the essential personal preparation, is to have the family circle united with Thomas and Wendsley in the ultimate 'party in heaven'.

Throughout their married lives God has been constantly surprising them with His promise to them of His provision for them. And Hertford and Phyllis are convinced He hasn't finished with them yet.

What else could He possibly have in store to challenge or brighten their future years?

Chapter 38

SOME PARTY ON EARTH

Shortly after they were married Ford brought his new bride to live in the bungalow which had once been home to him. When Hertford and Phyllis moved out in 2004 they let it, and when the former tenants moved out, Ford and Nicola moved in.

This was a special experience for the recently married man. He had spent the first 19 years of his life in that bungalow. It was where, as a child, he helped care for his handicapped brothers, Thomas and Wendsley. It was from the kitchen of this bungalow that his mum set out one day with a tray of trifles to try and sell them. It held so many precious memories for him, and now as a husband he was commencing married life in it.

If moving into the Donacloney bungalow was special for Ford and Nicola it was extra-special for his grandparents, Ford and Jean. The granny who had acted as mummy for so many years was pleased to see her grandson at the other end of the lane once more, with his lovely wife. Her husband, Ford senior, was absolutely thrilled to have a third generation of Arnolds 'down in the yard'. When Ford and Nicola were moving in 'granny Jean' was speaking to Phyllis, her daughter-in law, about the new occupants of the 'home' bungalow one day, and remarked, "If you had given the granda a million pounds he wouldn't be any happier!"

On Monday 12th November 2012, Ford left his new home which had once been his old home, with his wife Nicola, to make the short cross-country drive to the house which he left to get married, Killaney Lodge.

Hertford and Phyllis arrived back from a church meeting around 10pm and were surprised to find Ford's jeep sitting at the front of the house. When they had parked, Hertford strode on into the house to welcome whoever had called to see them, just slightly worried that some problem had arisen, perhaps with the business.

Phyllis, though, had her own secret thoughts about the unexpected visit. As she closed the courtyard gates to keep the dogs in for the night, she shared her aspirations with God. "Lord, wouldn't it be something if they were here to give us good news!" she said.

She neither expected nor received a divine response to her wishful musing and so crossed to the back door. Stopping, with her hand on the handle, Phyllis considered bouncing in and shouting, "It's great to see you both! Have you any good news for us?" but thought better of it. A second, more controlled, line of thinking held her back. "Catch yourself on, Phyllis. You are the mother and mother-in-law here," it counselled. "You are supposed to act all calm and sensible."

That is how she entered the house and greeted Ford and Nicola, all calm and sensible.

"It's lovely to see you both this evening," she said with genuine enthusiasm. "It's quite a surprise to have you over at this time of night."

"Yes, I suppose it is a bit of a surprise," Ford agreed, "but we've got our wedding video and thought you would like to see it."

Phyllis was terribly disappointed. Her mouth said, "That's great, son. I'll make a cup of coffee and then we can watch it together."

Her heart said, "A video! Who cares about a video?"

When his mum had made the coffee and they were about to have it while watching the video, Ford asked, "Where's Matthew?"

"He will be up in his bedroom, probably playing his

X-box," Phyllis informed him. "Why do you ask?"

Before she could even voice the opinion that Matthew might not be 'all that mad about watching a wedding video,' Ford was on his way up the stairs.

He must have had tremendous powers of persuasion for in a couple of minutes he was back down in the living room, with his younger brother following a few steps behind.

Ford crossed immediately to the TV and inserted a video from the bag he had been carrying around since he came in. No picture appeared on the screen but there was a sudden fanfare of trumpets. Phyllis thought she recognised the music. It was the fanfare of a film company.

"Do you not think that music is a bit loud for a wedding video, Ford?" she asked in all seriousness.

Then, turning to her husband for a second opinion, she said, "What do you think, Hertford? Is that not just a wee bit over the top?"

The bemused father hadn't even time to reply before Ford spoke again. He couldn't carry on the act any longer. "The truth of the matter is, mum and dad, there is no wedding video. We are sorry for telling you a wee white lie and leading you along, but this is why we have come," he announced.

With his back to the TV and the music still blaring in the background he turned his attention to the bag in his hand. All eyes were on him as he drew from it, ever so slowly, agonisingly slowly for his rapt audience, a tiny first-size Babygro.

"This is really why we have come over to see you tonight," Ford confessed at last. "We are expecting a baby next year and wanted you to be the first to hear the news! We know you are working with Noel to get your book out again and thought this might be something interesting to include!"

The last sentence was lost in the whoops of joy from Phyllis. She had by that time jumped up and was hugging the glowing with pride, but just slightly embarrassed, Nicola, as hard as she could. Words like 'marvellous, wonderful, brilliant, fabulous and fantastic' tumbled out of her mouth in no particular order.

Hertford was only slightly more restrained. He put his arm round Ford and congratulated him while waiting for Phyllis to release Nicola. When she did, he hugged Nicola and his wife concentrated on half-choking their older son.

Matthew wasn't quite sure how seventeen year old uncles-to-be were supposed to react in such a situation but he did his best. If there was somebody free to hug, he hugged them, and if there wasn't he just jumped up and down anyway. This appeared to be a very special party and it was easy enough to join the others in celebratory mode.

When the initial euphoria simmered down to mere bubbling excitement, the remainder of the evening was spent talking about baby topics. Phyllis had so much to ask about how Nicola was keeping and when she was going for appointments and scans. It was all dates and times and so thrilling to hear.

Before they left for home, Ford passed a remark which brought tears to the eyes of his mum and dad. "I looked into the nursery one day not so long ago," he told them, "and I thought, that's where Thomas and Wendsley used to sleep. It will soon be used again. We are going to make it our baby's nursery next year."

Reflecting on that nursery over in Donacloney brought back many memories for his parents, some joyful, some painful.

Now, though, the news they had just heard created an updated image in their minds. The same bungalow, the same nursery, another baby.

God, in His wisdom and grace, had turned the wheel full circle.

Now their son was looking forward to being a father.

And Hertford and Phyllis were, in the will of the Lord, to become grandparents!